Praise for This Edition

"*Expressive Writing: Counseling and Healthcare* provides a bridge in the much-needed world of psychological healing. It reminds us that creative approaches can provide breakthrough methods for clients to find their way to health. Spanning the diverse fields of poetry, journal therapy, spirituality, brain science, theories of self and much more, this book gives proof that expressive writing addresses a full spectrum of mental health challenges." —**Deborah Bowman**, PhD, dean of the graduate school of psychology, Naropa University; author of *The Female Buddha: Discovering the Heart of Liberation and Love*

"An exciting read that had me writing creatively even during the theory section; an inspiration to be more 'playful, spontaneous, and generous' with expressing ourselves and supporting others to do the same. This is a book that encompasses social, neurological, and practical ways of employing expressive writing. It is ideal for students, practitioners, and academic courses. I particularly liked the idea of writing with the focus on rewiring, reviving and healing neural pathways and the chapter on the significance and role of silence. I will definitely be adding *Expressive Writing: Counseling and Healthcare* to our reading list!" —**Claire Williamson**, MA, program leader for MSc, Creative Writing for Therapeutic Purposes, Metatonia Institute, Bristol and London; author of *The Soulwater Pool* and *Ride On*

"Thompson and Adams have gathered a rare collection of experts in the field who will bring this work to new audiences. The publication of original research material gives depth to the broadening field of expressive writing as a therapeutic modality. This book straddles the Atlantic with leaders in the field from the UK and the United States, making it truly international in scope. This is an inspiring collection of chapters, edited into a coherent volume from the broad overview in the introduction to the existential epilogue." —**Betty Cannon**, PhD, president, Boulder Psychotherapy Institute; author of *Sartre and Psychoanalysis*

"Write on! This collection offers clear, congruent, and creative guidelines from senior practitioners on important clinical topics. This substantive series

is a superbly curated resource for counselors, psychotherapists, and other helping professionals at all levels of experience. Highly recommended."
—**Barry M. Cohen**, ATR-BC; founder, Expressive Therapies Summit; co-founder, Mid-Atlantic Play Therapy Training Institute

"In 1990, trailblazer Kathleen Adams's *Journal to the Self* offered thrilling ideas about expressive writing that opened up new frontiers. More than a quarter-century later, Adams and Kate Thompson bring us to the edge of even newer frontiers of writing and healing in this collection of the latest exciting theories and practices. The authors in this book enlighten us with their research, their clinical work, and their theoretical understandings illustrating how writing offers relief, positive change, hope and zest.

In an outstanding chapter, Deborah Ross outlines neurophysiologic processes and how writing affects the brain. Drawing from the latest brain science, she presents with startling clarity how writing helps to establish and create neurological connections that bring about resilience, insight, and inspiration. Ross provides beautiful examples that enable the reader to translate complex theory into practical and enjoyable methods of working with clients.

All authors describe their work with specific insight, curiosity, and presence, honoring complexity while providing writing tools that offer light and companionship along the healing journey. This book gives detailed and clear examples of how to use expressive writing techniques as doors to well-being by providing a means to both listen to oneself and to affect positive change."
—**Wendi Kaplan**, LCSW, assistant clinical professor, George Washington University School of Medicine

"This bubbling fountain of inspiration feeds us with . . . serious and playful journal writing strategies to help clients and patients." —**Gillie Bolton**, PhD, author of *The Writer's Key: Introducing Creative Solutions for Life*

"The chapters in this remarkable volume comprise a treasure trove of innovative ideas and a breadth of relevant information of real value to a wide array of readers at all levels of experience. Thanks to the skill of the editors and authors, the clear, engaging prose in this collection not only makes ideas and applications comprehensible and useful to readers who are professionally trained and experienced in providing mental health counseling, but to any individual who wishes to support others in need, or indeed, strengthen their own coping process under stress.

I am impressed, in particular, with the inclusion of chapters addressing the newly understood neurobiological bases for the role of expressive writing in creating positive changes—not only in thought patterns but in building neuronal networks, strengthening immune function, and reducing physical symptoms of illness. This important understanding is described and explained in clear language that is based on cutting-edge research, yet remains accurate without being distorted by being oversimplified.

I whole-heartedly recommend this book as a source of healing and insight to any individual wishing to create and strengthen resilient coping mechanisms when experiencing a personal health or emotional crisis, or as a powerful resource for professionals seeking to help others." —**Mary Sue Moore**, PhD, licensed psychologist; Clinical Faculty, Boulder (CO) Institute for Psychotherapy and Research; hon. senior psychotherapist, child and family, Tavistock Clinic, London, England

"Can therapeutic writing help with brain injury, a diagnosis of cancer, or the isolation that can accompany deafness? Can poetry heal us? Can expressive writing cause the brain, quite literally, to change? In this extraordinary collection of essays, counselors and therapists on the frontier of therapeutic writing share their tools, processes, and the results they have achieved with their clients. Had I not already been a convert to the power of the pen, this groundbreaking book would have made me one." —**Mary Reynolds Thompson**, CAPF, CJF, author of *Reclaiming the Wild Soul: How Earth's Landscapes Restore Us to Wholeness*

Expressive Writing

Counseling and Healthcare

EDITED BY
KATE THOMPSON AND KATHLEEN ADAMS

Foreword by Christina Baldwin

ROWMAN & LITTLEFIELD
Lanham • Boulder • New York • London

Published by Rowman & Littlefield
A wholly owned subsidiary of The Rowman & Littlefield Publishing Group, Inc.
4501 Forbes Boulevard, Suite 200, Lanham, Maryland 20706
www.rowman.com

Unit A, Whitacre Mews, 26-34 Stannary Street, London SE11 4AB

British Library Cataloguing in Publication Information Available

Library of Congress Cataloging-in-Publication Data Available

ISBN 978-1-4758-0772-1 (cloth : alk. paper) — ISBN 978-1-4758-0773-8 (pbk. : alk. paper) — ISBN 978-1-4758-0774-5 (electronic)

♾™ The paper used in this publication meets the minimum requirements of American National Standard for Information Sciences—Permanence of Paper for Printed Library Materials, ANSI/NISO Z39.48-1992.

Printed in the United States of America

Contents

Section 2: Practice

Epilogue

Series Overview: About the *It's Easy to W.R.I.T.E.* Expressive Writing Series

Expressive writing originates from the writer's lived experience—the past, present, or imagined future life. Written in the author's own voice, expressive writing creates bridges between thought and feeling, reason and intuition, idea and action. It is equally rooted in language arts and social science, and it takes multiple forms: journals, poetry, life story, personal essay, creative nonfiction, song lyrics, notes, and snippets of thought. Expressive writing is democratic and accessible. No special knowledge is needed, supplies are available and affordable, and research confirms that outcomes can be profound and even life-changing.

The *It's Easy to W.R.I.T.E.* Expressive Writing Series captures the voices of worldwide experts on the power of writing for personal development, academic improvement, and lasting behavioral change. Authors are both theorists and practitioners of the work they document, bringing real-life examples of practical techniques and stories of actual outcomes.

Individually or as a compendium, the volumes in the *It's Easy to W.R.I.T.E.* Expressive Writing Series represent thoughtful, innovative, demonstrated approaches to the myriad ways life-based writing can shape both critical thinking and emotional intelligence. Books in the series are designed to have versatile appeal for classroom teachers and administrators, health and behavioral health professionals, graduate programs that prepare educators and counselors, facilitators of expressive writing, and individuals who themselves write expressively. Workbooks offer well-crafted, self-paced writing programs for individual users, with facilitation guides and curricula for anyone who wishes to organize peer-writing circles to explore the material in community.

Each book or chapter author is held to exacting standards set by the series editor, Kathleen Adams, who, prior to her 1985 launch as a pioneer and global expert in the expressive writing field, was trained as a journalist and served as chief editor for a small nonfiction publishing company.

It's Easy to W.R.I.T.E.

*W*hat do you want to write about? Name it. Write it down. (If you don't know, try one of these: *What's going on? How do I feel? What's on my mind? What do I want? What's the most important thing to do? What's the best/worst thing right now?*)

*R*econnect with your center. Close your eyes. Take three deep breaths. Focus. Relax your body and mind. Gather your thoughts, feelings, questions, ideas.

*I*nvestigate your thoughts and feelings. Start writing and keep writing. Follow the pen/keyboard. If you get stuck, close your eyes and recenter yourself. Reread what you've already written and continue. Try not to edit as you go; that can come later, if at all.

*T*ime yourself. Write for five to twenty minutes or whatever time you choose. Set the timer on your phone, stove, or computer. Plan another three to five minutes at the end for reflection.

*E*xit smart. Reread what you've written and reflect on it in a sentence or two: *As I read this, I notice . . .* or *I'm aware of . . .* or *I feel . . .* Note any action steps you might take or any prompts you might use for additional writes.

Foreword

The Self as the Source of the Story

Words are magic. We cannot imagine our world, or our lives, or how to relate, without the use of language. Spoken word, written word—we language ourselves into being.

When I was three years old, I was helping my mother set the table for a large family gathering, mostly adults. My grandmother called from the kitchen, "We're sixteen for dinner, counting Chrissie."

"Chrissie doesn't count," my mother replied—thinking of the table space.

"Oh, yes I do!" I countered, "One-two-three-four—." Adults laughed. Words make us real to ourselves: we are seen through words, understood or misunderstood. We take our place through language. We weave a narrative of belonging and differentiation within our family, school, community, religion, ethnicity, gender, and society. We encode experiences through language: we link experiences through story. We become the source of our stories.

This ability to live in the interactive matrix of our own self-storytelling is a hugely powerful neurological, psychological, and spiritual function. We make up what something means, and then over time we discover if this story is helpful or harmful to our ongoing journey of selfhood and relationship. We are not only the source of our stories—we are the sorcerers of our stories. We have the power to change the story to heal our ways forward. It is this power that is taught and explored in this fine collection of essays.

By age nine I had decided I wanted to be a writer. At age twelve I began my first diary—a practice that has continued nearly unbroken for the past fifty-plus years. This choice, made by a rather shy seventh grader, is probably the most formative life decision I ever made. Writing down words adds dimensions of significance, selection, and sorting to the story-flow of the mind. It is this potent alchemy that contributors to *Expressive Writing: Counseling and Healthcare*, understand and share with readers.

I have written about and taught journal writing and creative nonfiction for forty years and watched the field of study and understanding about why this works emerge and grow. Kay Adams and Kate Thompson are reliable and wise leaders in this exploration, and they have pulled together a solid array of contributors.

Millions of people write journals—because we can, because literacy is freedom, because we dare to speak truth to ourselves—and there are people, thankfully, devoting significant parts of their lives to understanding this impulse, framing it, putting a context around it, adding the science. Reading this book is a gift to those who want to know more about how writing works, and why story is such a powerful map toward wholeness.

Christina Baldwin
June 2015

Books by Christina Baldwin

Storycatcher, Making Sense of Our Lives through the Power and Practice of Story (2007)

Life's Companion, Journal Writing as a Spiritual Practice (1991, 2007)

One to One, Self Understanding through Journal Writing (1978, 1991)

Preface

KATHLEEN ADAMS

The last time public awareness about expressive writing took a big step forward was April 1999, when the *Journal of the American Medical Association* published a study that asked patients with rheumatoid arthritis or asthma to write about "the most stressful experience of your life" for three consecutive days, for about fifteen or twenty minutes each time. At a four-month follow-up, 47 percent of the test patients (compared to 24 percent of the control patients) "met criteria for clinically relevant improvement" in their chronic diseases. "This is the first study to demonstrate that writing about stressful life experiences improves physician ratings of disease severity," said Joshua Smyth and colleagues. "These gains were beyond those attributable to the standard medical care that all participants were receiving" (Smyth et al. 1999).

The public's awareness and interest was raised not so much by the study itself but by the unprecedented media coverage it received. It was an early experience of "going viral." For months, the science, psychology, and health news across all media was saturated with reports on the health benefits of expressive writing. Suddenly, instead of being an obscure topic of interest to researchers and expressive writers, people all over the world began to notice and talk about the idea that one might actually improve physical health through writing thoughts and feelings in a notebook or on a computer screen. The concept of expressive writing for healthier, better living began to become normalized, a process that continues to this day.

The same week that *JAMA* published the Smyth study, Louise DeSalvo's book *Writing as a Way of Healing* made its debut to immediate critical acclaim. DeSalvo, a writing professor at Hunter College, explored how the creative process can be a portal to emotional healing of the "wounded psyche" and "wounded body." She writes:

> What, though, if writing weren't such a luxury? What if writing were a simple, significant, yet necessary way to achieve spiritual, emotional, and psychic wholeness? To synthesize thought and feeling, to understand how feeling relates to events in our lives and vice versa? What if writing were as important and as basic a function and as significant to maintaining and promoting our psychic and physical wellness as, say, exercise, healthful food, pure water, clean air, rest and repose, and some soul-satisfying practice? (DeSalvo 1999, 6)

Two significant publications contemporaneously delivered parallel messages to a curious public: Expressive writing is a way of contributing to the improvement of both physical and emotional health. The combination represented a major shift in the collective consciousness about writing and healing.

In the intervening years, research has continued in the now-classic Pennebaker paradigm, with studies of interest from around the globe. Credentials training programs have emerged to prepare the next generation of journal therapists and facilitators. More and more people are turning to writing for stress management, life review, and emotional regulation. Digital journaling has grown roots and wings; a study reports that those who participated in a thirty-day digital journaling challenge reported no significant difference in the results gained from keyboarded or handwritten journals (Adams, Ohren, and Hudson 2015).

A recent focus (and perhaps the next big shift) is the relationship between expressive writing and what Deborah Ross (chapter 2, "Your Brain on Ink") calls "self-directed neuroplasticity." Several other chapter authors also share their thinking about the intersection of writing and neuroscience. The emerging work will take up the study of how a purposeful and intentional program of expressive writing designed specifically around self-directed or practitioner-guided goals for healing, growth, and change can create neural pathways that over time may literally change the brain.

One new trend is assured: In the coming decade, the next generation of practitioners will take up the baton and be the authors, leaders, and spokespeople for the field. As you will see in these pages (and indeed, in all books in this series), the field of expressive writing will be in very good hands indeed.

What You Will Learn

We begin with a call into community by two long-time colleagues, Graham Hartill and certified poetry therapist Victoria Field. They invite us into rich conversation about why we do this work (Victoria: "My main interest these days is in the hinterland between health and illness and what happens in self-referral, open-ended writing groups") and how the work shapes us (Graham: "I find myself asking again, what is it, to 'make whole'? Isn't it a grand ambition? And how can writing help do it? . . . Thus I find myself working in a continual state of questioning."). Their generous dialogue demonstrates that we are all "In This Together."

What happens to "Your Brain on Ink?" That's the question that certified journal therapist Deborah Ross explores in a synthesis of the science of neuroplasticity and the practice of expressive writing. A graduate of both the Mindsight Institute and the Therapeutic Writing Institute, Deborah uniquely understands the intersection between writing and brain change. She calls this *self-directed neuroplasticity*—"a method of accelerating experience-dependent neurological change through expressive writing." It's exciting new thinking, articulated in print for the first time.

From the cutting edge of brain science to the cutting edge of research, the team of John Evans, Karen Jooste, Meredith Mealer, and Marc Moss takes us behind the scenes for an up-close look at a research project. "Expressive Writing for Caregiver Resilience: A Research Perspective" details a twelve-week writing intervention, an online adaptation of John's face-to-face groups that he offers through Duke University Integrative Medicine. Of particular interest: John's six-part model is the first extension of the classic Pennebaker paradigm, which typically concludes after three or four writing episodes within the same week.

Creating art from the ashes of trauma is a profound, even life-changing, process. In "Writing the Darkness: The Transformative Writing Model," Sherry Reiter brings her significant expertise with writing through all manner of life crises. She offers ten principles of trauma-based transformative writing and three compelling case studies that demonstrate and validate her thinking.

Beth Jacobs closes the *Theory* section with a thoughtful study of "Emotional Balance, the Journal, and the Therapy Session." "I listened carefully to [client] descriptions of their journals and why they were writing. The common theme was . . . emotional expression," Beth writes. "Journals were containing emotion that had nowhere to go." Together with her signature theme of writing for emotional balance (she's a pioneer), Beth also explores multiplicity of self, writing interactively with a client, creating writing rituals, releasing emotional blockages, and the journal as transitional space.

The second section, *Practice*, opens with "WOWSA! Play-Based Journal Therapy." Registered play therapist and award-winning trauma-informed therapist Cherie Spehar wows us with a fountain of creative possibilities for playing with words and writing instruments, all structured around her title acronym. Brimming with sensible ideas about the synergy of writing and play, Cherie breaks new ground across the disciplines.

Carol Ross infuses "Therapeutic Writing in Psychiatric Care" with a remarkable transparency, highlighting the interventions and strategies she uses for expressive writing in both acute and intensive psychiatric care hospital units. Particularly strong are her case studies, each vibrant with compassion and dignity.

"Her eyes would not leave the page that was scribbled with lines and words—the first real evidence that her story had not only been 'heard' and understood, but now recorded, made real and tangible. When she finally looked at me, the tears started to flow and she said—with her hands—'Show this to my mom so she can know me.'" So begins Donna Houston's "Now That I See: Journaling with Deaf Teens," a compelling story of locked-inside stories made visible through scribing and other interactive forms of expressive writing.

In "Roots of Resilience: Writing for Practitioner Self-Care," Susan Smith Pierce, director of professional development and training and internship supervision for a large, multi-location family counseling agency, offers six pathways to radical self-care, each with its own set of writing prompts. "We know that journal writing is an immediate, effective, accessible, and useful stress management practice," Susan writes. "What we perhaps haven't fully appreciated is the role our journals can play in building resilience and activating our coping strengths."

"Creating a New Story after Brain Injury" is the hard, painful task of anyone who has undergone traumatic brain injury (TBI). Certified journal facilitator Barbara Stahura, caregiver for her husband after a motorcycle accident, wrote her way through his rehabilitation and then created TBI writing groups for a local hospital. In this chapter, abundant with resources, she writes about the program that helps brain-injured people create their new stories.

In "After the Deep Dive: Reflections on Writing beyond Cancer," oncology social worker and certified journal therapist Jean Rowe shares the expressive writing programs she has developed for cancer survivors. Existential themes of loss, identity, and survival weave through her rich case studies and facilitation plans, each infused with Jean's signature brand of grit, art, and grace.

The book ends with a meditation on "Honoring Silence." In their epilogue, Kate Thompson and Jeannie Wright discuss possible meanings of not-writing and silence on the page, considering silence as both potential and deprivation, and exploring how writers and therapists have used it to profound effect.

Who Is This Book For?

There are several audiences for this book: counselors and therapists; health care professionals; university programs that offer coursework in primary care and counseling; practitioners and facilitators; and writers who know or are discovering the power of expressive writing for healing, growth, and change.

If you are a counselor or therapist, you will have a resource guide for best-practice facilitation of expressive writing in private practice, school counseling, or agency work.

If you are a health care professional, you will find new research methods, ideas for inpatient hospital groups, and writing interventions for populations such as those recovering from traumatic brain injury or cancer—all both creative and compassionate.

If you are university faculty in education, social sciences, or guidance/counseling, this text offers a comprehensive look at interdisciplinary ways in which the authenticity of expressive writing can be incorporated into a holistic philosophy of classroom and community practice.

If you are a credentialed practitioner, community-based facilitator, writing coach, creative writing teacher, or other who brings this work to the world, you have guidance and role-modeling from master teachers whose programs can bring insight and awareness to your work.

Expressive Writing: Counseling and Health Care

In 1985 I called my first journal circle. Six of my friends sat on my living-room floor and wrote their hearts out and shared their stories. I was a first-semester graduate student in a counseling program, and I knew in that instant that the intersection of personal healing and journal writing was my life's work.

I have always done my work in community. I am a natural weaver of lives. I am a gatherer of overlapping, intersecting circles of those who speak on the page, who read their stories in voices that quaver or whisper or soar, in the presence of witnesses who receive without judgment and respond with compassion.

This is what I have learned in writing circles across the decades and around the world: Expressive writing changes us. It brings peace to our hearts. It restores balance. Writing connects us to the parts of ourselves that have been lost, abandoned, neglected, forgotten, or ignored. We learn that there are wise, friendly, and reasonable aspects of ourselves that want us to succeed. These "best selves" are willing to share their wisdom with us. Writing is the bridge.

Community also changes us. We learn that we are not alone. We see ourselves reflected in another's compassionate eyes. We hold for each other what we cannot reliably hang onto for ourselves. We learn that we are enough, we are sufficient, we have something to say and a voice with which to say it.

Pennebaker states that "expressive writing has the potential to change the way you see the world" (2013, xiv). I believe that writing communities—in classrooms, conference rooms, family rooms, therapists' offices, places of worship, community centers, coffee shops—have the power to deepen and accelerate the process of change. What might arise, I wonder, from a collectively shifted world view?

My vision for this book, and indeed the series, is that it will substantially advance the dialogue about the role of expressive writing for healing, growth, and change at every level of body, mind, and spirit: in the mirror, at the dinner table, in the therapy chair, at the doctor's office, in the classroom, at the place of worship, throughout the community, into the culture.

I welcome you to the community formed by those who read this book, and I invite you to join the conversation.

Kathleen Adams MA, LPC
Series Editor, *It's Easy to W.R.I.T.E.* Expressive Writing Series
June 2015

Join the conversation:
www.itseasytowrite.com
kathleen@itseasytowrite.com

References

Adams, Kathleen, Nathan Ohren, and Brenda Hudson. 2015. *The 30-day digital journal challenge: A report for helping professionals.* Wheat Ridge, CO: Center for Journal Therapy.

DeSalvo, Louise. 1999. *Writing as a way of healing: How telling our stories transforms our lives.* San Francisco: Harper.

Pennebaker, James. 2013. Foreword to *Expressive writing: Foundations of practice*, edited by Kathleen Adams. Lanham, MD: Rowman & Littlefield Education.

Smyth, Joshua, Arthur Stone, Adam Hurewitz, and Alan Kaell. 1999. Effects of writing about stressful experiences on symptom reduction in patients with asthma or rheumatoid arthritis: A randomized trial. *JAMA* 281(14). Accessed February 7, 2015. http://jama.jamanetwork.com/article.aspx?articleid=189437.

THEORY

1

In This Together

Writing in Health and Social Care

GRAHAM HARTILL AND VICTORIA FIELD

Graham: Well, we've been working together at Ty Newydd, the Writers' Centre for Wales, for eight years now, running our week-long residential courses in Writing in Health and Social Care. More than a hundred people have attended over that time, some with health issues of their own, and all wanting to explore the possibilities of how we can use creativity through words to help one another.

Apart from this great collaboration (long may it continue), we've worked separately in a wide variety of locations with all kinds of people. Speaking for myself, I started out working with people with mental health issues and spent several years working with elderly people in my role as community outreach writer with the Ledbury Poetry Festival as well as working alongside disabled people using creative writing and cross-art form activities as ways to express disability issues in the public domain. I am now in a post as a writer-in-residence in a prison, the permanency of which makes it a rare position. All of this experience brings me face to face with people who are living life in the deep end.

I'm also proud to be a member of the team that delivers the MSc in Creative Writing for Therapeutic Purposes for the Metanoia Institute. There, I find myself continually exploring with my colleagues the varied applications of creative writing in settings where the term *therapeutic* is applied in the broad sense and recognized in terms of social as well as personal conditions.

We look at issues to do with personal liberation, identity, and self-esteem through genres such as reflexive writing, poetic inquiry, narrative inquiry, and autobiographical fiction, all techniques we bring to our work at Ty Newydd, of course. I like to think that our creative abilities, our *authorship*, goes hand in hand with our sense of personal *authority*.

Victoria: "Creativity through words to help one another" is a good summary of therapeutic writing. I am often struck by how a diverse group of people, such as those coming to our courses, can find connections through expressive writing and sharing that writing. Ty Newydd operates an open-door policy, and we know that most of the participants come with both a professional and a personal interest in the field. On the one hand, they may be working as counselors, therapists, doctors, nurses, librarians, or teachers and think therapeutic writing may have useful applications. On the other hand, they have either discovered, or intuited, that writing can help make sense of events in their lives.

There is perhaps a difference between the writing that happens in self-referral groups—such as Ty Newydd—and closed settings where people are not free to leave. I am thinking of prisons, where you have much experience, or work I have done in care homes, a day hospital for psychiatric patients, and on a stroke rehabilitation unit. There, people may be in crisis, or at risk of severe depression, self-harm, or even suicide, experiencing what you call the "deep end" of life.

My main interest these days is in the hinterland between health and illness and what happens in self-referral, open-ended writing groups. I worked for three years running a Words for Wellbeing group at Falmouth Health Centre in Cornwall, UK, aimed at people with mental health problems such as mild depression or anxiety. Their difficulties were often due to life circumstances such as bereavement, or social isolation because of care-giving responsibilities.

Some people had physical conditions that were depressing because of pain or physical limitations, such as MS, ME (chronic fatigue syndrome), or arthritis. Others had diagnoses of severe and enduring mental illness. Although the group met at the Health Centre, and there was a link to the General Practitioner's office, there was no need for anyone to disclose a diagnosis.

Similarly, I have just completed a one-year, self-referral poetry therapy group that met weekly at the Beaney (a public library and gallery in the center of Canterbury). The group was billed as "Wise Words for Wellbeing" and was promoted through health networks. It was set up with an antistigma agenda that meant that no one had to declare a diagnosis and was intended to be therapeutic without being therapy.

Nevertheless, and gradually, individuals disclosed details of their medical histories. These included stroke, brain injury, diagnoses of depression, eating disorders, OCD, and inpatient stays on a psychiatric ward. As stories emerged in the safety and permissiveness of the writing group, there came references to traumas such as rape, domestic abuse, bereavements (including two women bereaved of grandchildren), as well as ongoing challenges such as caring for sick relatives, work-related stress, fertility problems, divorce, housing difficulties, and adjusting to disability.

With one or two exceptions, none of these diagnoses or difficulties were apparent on first meeting. We were all first and foremost human beings participating in a writing group to improve our health and well-being. Everyone was functioning in society, even while suffering. The Words for Wellbeing group was a place to give voice to all aspects of human experience, its complexity, the joy and the pain.

Graham: And the question is always there: If a person is not healthy in the normal sense of the word (and I'm thinking specifically about mental health here), how can writing be helpful? I guess we'll be looking at various answers to that question in this conversation, but I'd like to continue by referring to a paper I wrote for one of the pioneering books in our field, *The Self on the Page*. I begin by saying that

> In their origins, the words "poetry" and "healing" have a lot in common; "poetry" comes from the Greek and means to compose, to pull things together, to shape, to create, to make; less well-known is the etymology of "healing," which derives from the ancient Germanic khailaz, through Anglo-Saxon hoelan, which also means to make whole. (Hartill 1998)

Looking back now, I find myself asking again, what is it, to "make whole"? Isn't it a grand ambition? And how can writing help do it? After all, we might be talking about people with incurable dementia, with depression or cancer, or perhaps the sufferers of some terrible parental or institutional neglect who have gone on to inflict some related torment on others. Are we not begging the central question: Can such a person ever be "whole" again?

Thus I find myself working in a continual state of questioning. More basically, I find myself in a state of always meeting; meeting the questions, yes, but, more simply, meeting the person or people in front of me: the newly admitted prisoner in his cell, pacing up and down to dispel his fear or disbelief; the elderly woman sipping tea, surrounded by other elderly men and women, day in, day out; or the course participant, who has made a commitment to finding out how words can be put to use. But always it's a meeting with myself, which is an interesting, if sometimes troubling, experience.

The work is rarely, if ever, boring: it continually challenges and re-creates what writing is, and brings us daily to an account of the meaning of life and death. I'm not being fanciful here: we work with the meaning of life and death. This is one kind of answer to the question of "making whole." And I don't mean to be pretentious, it's just that, like medicine, this is what art does, habitually.

Victoria: I think you have hit the nail on the head when you say that "writing brings us daily to an account of the meaning of life and death." In what might be called a post-religious society, people can struggle with those big questions about existence and it is not clear to whom we can turn to explore them openly.

As you alluded, questioning is at the heart of therapeutic writing. At Ty Newydd, where we offer both the experience of therapeutic writing and a chance to reflect on the processes involved, I often share a quotation from Rilke's *Letters to a Young Poet* (2012). The young poet is wondering about love, but Rilke's answer is relevant to life in general. He advises his correspondent to

> have patience with everything that is unsolved in your heart and try to cherish the questions themselves, like closed rooms and like books written in a very strange tongue. . . . Do not search now for the answers which cannot be given you because you could not live them. It is a matter of living everything. Live the questions now.

Often at the beginning of a course, or in the early stages of a writing group, there is an impatience to learn techniques instantly or to find resolution. Writing is iterative and provisional and can be a creative and transformative way of staying with confusion, pain, and ambivalence without rushing to "fix" it.

Healing is an aspiration common to the arts and medicine. Writing, like all the arts, is holistic, nuanced, unresolved, and open. In that respect, it is complementary to mainstream medicine, which has become increasingly specialized, some would say fragmented. In psychiatry, particularly with the proliferation of so-called disorders in the new DSM-5, there has been a tendency to pathologize what previously might be considered a normal reaction to life events. The British Psychological Society and American Psychological Association have expressed concern as outlined in the Society Statement on DSM-5 published online (2011).

For a doctor, concerned to alleviate suffering in the patient, it is easier to diagnose "depression," and prescribe accordingly, than to contend with loneliness, grief, or despair. James Davies argues that psychiatry, once reserved for "only the most distressed members of society," has now "crashed through the walls of the hospital and surged into every corner of contemporary life" (2013, 2). Prescriptions for antidepressant drugs by doctors in primary care have increased enormously in the United Kingdom, and the rate of prescribing is even higher in the United States. Davies argues that many patients are not "mad" (or arguably even "ill") but "just like you and me. Average people simply trying to make their way" (2013, 2).

Someone trying to make his way can find writing helpful in that process. The metaphor of life's journey underpins much work in poetry therapy. For example, Fiona Hamilton describes how

> a train journey offers an objective correlative for the writing process. The varying rhythms of acceleration and slowing, like the rhythms of language negotiating sense. . . . The intermittent pauses and somewhere, not necessarily where you expected, the final stop, where you will re-emerge into the world, changed. (2011, 211)

For me, therapeutic writing is more about "care" than "cure." Some experiences of trauma and loss will never be fully healed (analogous to living with disability after, say, a stroke or an accident), but writing can give meaning to the experience and contain it. The writing workshop itself acts as a container, a safe space, and a sanctuary. Participants' comments on what they valued on the Wise Words for Wellbeing project include

- To be among different people for whom it is natural to think about thinking, poetry, language, and feelings, and for whom it is normal to use writing as a tool.
- To be more of myself, by being in the group. Self-understanding, and compassion for others, is increased.
- My creative capacity is very important to me emotionally. I am able to express myself in the writing group without my disability proving a hindrance.
- "Me time" to reconnect to my true feelings and have a dialogue with myself. A chance simply to do one thing without distraction. (Field 2014)

A common theme here is connection, to self, others, and the inner life. Building such connections is an ongoing process. A participant in my Wise Words for Wellbeing group writes of "beginning to find joy again." None of them specifically mentioned their "health" (or illness) concern.

Their comments fit well with the current health agenda that talks about "living well with" long-term conditions (LTC). An LTC is defined on a British government website as "a health problem that can't be cured but can be controlled by medication or other therapies. . . . [The figure for LTCs] is set to increase over the next ten years, particularly those people with three or more conditions at once. Examples of long-term conditions include high blood pressure, depression, dementia and arthritis" (Department of Health 2013).

I think we need to move away from a single idea of what "healthy" might mean to one who embraces the multiplicity of human experience, which will, especially with increasing life expectancy, include living with disease. Mood disorders such as depression can exacerbate problems with other health concerns. My personal belief is that therapeutic writing improves health by elevating mood and possibly, as Pennebaker (2004) would claim, removing the stress caused by repressing thoughts and emotions.

We have set out some general philosophical context—and posed several questions. Shall we move toward some specifics? Would you like to give some examples from your practice, and I will do likewise?

Graham: Yes, there are two encounters that spring to mind, very different from one another, highlighting different issues within different contexts. One is to do with working with people in old age, the other to do with prisoners. Both may serve to expand our notion of health and well-being and the roles writing can play.

The first is a transcription piece from a conversation with a woman in a care home. "Jenny" was 102 and bright as a button. I met her on several occasions and was privileged to witness many of her life stories. This is a transcription poem from the collection *Lifelines* published with the Ledbury Poetry Festival (Hartill 2003). The first line nonplussed me somewhat, as you can imagine! But all became clear:

102

My stepfather was my boyfriend.
He was 19, I was 16,
And I went

When Father died
(he was never the same since the war)
He proposed to mother.
Then she died,
She was 49.

Then one day he came in the shop
And said right,
I'm going to marry you!
I said he blooming well wasn't!

He's over Hereford way.
I told them not to tell him
That Jenny was still alive.

Is old age or its frequent companion, dementia, a "health" issue, given that they're incurable? Can writing be therapeutic if the participant is on such a different wavelength from the writer, hardly aware that writing is going on at all and possibly unable to appreciate the outcome as "poem"? This is a much more contentious issue. My response to these and related questions is to request a reconfiguration of some basic terms, to make some further inquiries. What do we mean by "health," by "participation," by "therapeutic," and centrally, by "poem"?

I would include the notion of well-being within the larger concept of health. The concept of "living well" I like because of its range of concern, out beyond the pathology of the individual. When a person is approaching death, there may be no getting better physically, but life can still be lived to the fullest; that life can be valued, and be felt to be valued, not only by the participant herself but by her nearest and dearest and, through publication, by the world at large. That voice can be heard, and be heard as still having something interesting to say, and an interesting way of saying it.

I know from experience that this is enriching, and that the time of the actual encounter, the meeting between the writer and the participant, is at the heart of the experience. I feel justified in calling that a poetic event. The poem is not just the printed outcome, but the whole process, a process that continues after the individual poem is published and whose therapeutic benefit may be felt by many, specifically the family and loved ones of the participant.

Whether any printed outcome can be called a "poem" is perhaps a rather more academic question, but one worth lingering on for its therapeutic significance. Working at Ledbury, I would return to my collaborator a few days later with a typed-up text in hand and read it back to her. The economy of the transcribed poem, its accuracy and authenticity, its energy, coming directly from the words of the participant herself was almost always instantly recognized and appreciated. "That's my story!" "Those are my words!" would be common responses.

It's become a kind of unwritten rule about transcription poetry that however selective the transcriber is, one doesn't add his or her own words to the text. There may well be a case for doing so in different kinds of work, but here I was following this practice, as developed and applied most notably by John Killick (1998), recognizing a passage of speech that resonated with me and transcribing it in a poetic form, alert to form as much as to content. I make no bones about the fact that I am intervening, shaping a text from a spoken encounter, but the vitally important ethical act of sharing the text with the speaker, and getting her approval, amendments, or even rejection, is where we meet: the point of collaboration. She brings the words; I bring my poetic practice. The outcome needs to be satisfactory, and hopefully creatively joyful, to both parties.

A different kind of collaborative process and perhaps at a deeper and more individualistic therapeutic level, is evidenced by my second anecdote, this time involving a prisoner; I have called him Jim (Hartill 2011).

We had been working together for some time when one day he told me he wanted to write about his little brother, who had died, purportedly from measles, when still a child. They had shared a room and Jim had grown up with the belief, promulgated by his mother, that he had "given" his little brother the disease. Jim already had a list of possible titles for his piece. "Which one would you choose?" he asked.

"The Guardian Angel" I replied.

"I'm glad you said that."

Straightaway I had the feeling that Jim had already made an important, if subconscious, decision to challenge the guilt inherent in the imposed narrative of their relationship: Charlie as victim, Jim as killer. Instead of being his victim, Charlie now reassured him; Charlie was thus reconfigured—no longer the avenging angel but the guardian. Jim was about to forgive himself.

But the plot is thicker that than this. Jim had been abused as a child by a Catholic priest who was close to his mother. As a Catholic schoolboy, he was forbidden to write with his left hand, the left hand being the hand with which the devil wrote. In fact it wasn't until he came to prison that he felt free to write freehand at all, with his left hand, which now, paradoxically, was free. He undertook the therapeutic program and came to serious realizations about himself and what had led to his offending. Now he was ready to make one final and enormous recognition.

One morning, I found Jim, once suicidal, in an elated state. "The most incredible thing has happened. In the middle of writing this Guardian Angel piece, it came to me: maybe Charlie didn't die of measles at all! Maybe it was cot death or something. It could have been. Maybe it had nothing to do with me."

"Maybe not, Jim."

"It's incredible. All my life I've suffered from this guilt. And only now I can see how it was, through writing this."

Free hand: Jim was freed at that moment from his guilt-script, his Cain and Abel script. What I find fascinating is the symmetry of the symbols and events that bound him, and that led to his release: the abusing priest/the abusing victim; the hand of the "Devil"/the hand of "God"; the abusing hand of the priest/the free hand of the writer. In narrative terms, this seems rather more to me than rewriting the life-script; its central theme is writing itself, its central key (and I use the term advisedly): Jim was imprisoned in a story, and in a terrible silence (his abuse); its effects extended to his victims; when he became free to write with his natural hand, he became free to rewrite. His life, past, present, and hopefully future, thus became healthier.

Upon release, Jim went on to do an Open University Creative Writing course.

Victoria: I find those two case studies fascinating and demonstrate the "hall-of-mirrors" quality of therapeutic writing. Individuals are simultaneously engaging with you—the facilitator and listener, their own psyches in all their complexity, and pieces of writing that they may have produced, or the facilitator introduced. Each of these is subtly reflected and refracted through the process of formal engagement, and afterward, often unconsciously. Nothing is ever quite what it seems.

Your examples bring me back again to one of the characteristics of writing and poetry that make it, in my opinion, therapeutic. Poems and stories are provisional and can be rewritten and reread in a variety of ways. Jim's changing account of his brother's death is a startling example of restorying. He is no longer Cain murdering Abel, but an innocent bystander. As well as being protagonists in the drama of our own lives, we can also find ourselves in extant stories and myths. These are powerful resources for expressive writing. In my own work, people find stories such as those about Sleeping Beauty, John Bunyan's pilgrim, or Persephone entering the underworld, rich sources of insight. And again, these well-known stories can be made personal, remade and retold.

As you know, I trained with the International Federation for Biblio/Poetry Therapy, based in the United States. There are many variations of practice within the discipline, and my own work is usually with groups. I usually introduce a "poem" (shorthand for any text that can open an imaginative space), encourage reflection, and then invite writing in response. Nick Mazza (2003) has developed a "poetry therapy practice model" that has three components that can be summarized as the receptive/prescriptive component (introducing literature), the expressive/creative component (the participants' writing), and a symbolic/ceremonial component.

There is an increasing literature theorizing how reading and writing might be therapeutic, but it's important to emphasize that it is always multidimensional and holistic. It is impossible to isolate the variables in a writing workshop. Often the symbolic and ceremonial aspects—such as the room, how people sit, tea breaks, rituals of reading and writing—are as important as the activity itself.

A poem that I often use toward the end of a series of workshops, or at the end of a workshop day, is one by Penelope Shuttle called "When Happiness Returns after a Long Absence" (2010, 125). It is an extended metaphor describing the aftermath of a great grief and how "happiness" begins to return first as an ant, then as a beetle, and then as busy spider. The poet asks happiness to "raise its game" and finally become a wren, saying such "modest happiness" she can bear. Sharing this with a group, there's always a sigh of recognition. The poem gives permission for the reader to stay with sadness as long as necessary, and the animal metaphors are playful and poignant. I solicited written comments from one group and these included:

> This poem gave me a feeling of being set free. Free from the heavy weight of even breathing, after loss. It held huge respect for the time taken and the journey back to simply functioning again. Mel J. (Field 2012, 62)

I then ask the group to think of an animal metaphor for their own happiness—and then to "raise the game." This way of working with a metaphor can allow the participant to keep a safe distance from directly personal material until he or she is ready to work with it directly. Elaborating on the metaphor in writing can lead to real insights. In the group described above, metaphors for happiness included a buzzing bee ("Fly into my heart. . . . / Keep me connected to others and / Help me to be generous with your honey") and a puppy ("chew up unhappy thoughts, / Anxious thoughts, Angry thoughts / And poop them out behind the shed in a / Pile of smelly, steamy mess") (Field 2012, 63).

In times of difficulty, or when a person is depressed or anxious, there's often a tendency to engage in what have been labeled "cognitive distortions," which include polarized thinking, the idea that things are either all good or all bad, catastrophizing, self-blame, and so on. Writing groups in health and social care offer a forum where, through shared perceptions and writing, participants can develop more nuanced ways of thinking and treat themselves more kindly. Writing, especially poetry, actively encourages subtle interpretations and can be richly ambiguous. Things get interesting in a group when someone says, "I find that poem very sad," and someone else counters, "No, it's optimistic," and we begin exploring what's behind those perceptions. Life is seldom all wonderful or all dreadful.

When working in the community or in primary care, a maxim I often repeat to myself is that the task at hand is to "heal the past, live the present, and create the future." Therapeutic writing offers the potential to do all three. And this can be either concrete and literal, or metaphoric. For example, when working with Robert Frost's poem, "Fire and Ice" (1973), we can focus on memories of cold and warmth, we can engage with the current season, or we can use it to inform our own intentions, especially in terms of relationships and emotions such as desire and hate that are mentioned in the poem.

I have also had the opportunity to work one on one with individuals who have had strokes or diagnoses of dementia. In the latter case, linear ideas of time are irrelevant and the focus is very much on "care" and living well, or as well as possible, with conditions that are not curable. Here, the writing is very much in the here and now, engaging with the senses, the seasons, and often a sense of the eternal. Rather than exploring and attempting to resolve issues, writing can act as a way of giving solace, accepting things as they are. This links very closely with the increasingly established use of mindfulness techniques in health and social care.

Graham: Yes, Vicky, thanks for reminding us about the wider picture, the broad sweep of being in this world and how artistic work in words can enrich it, at all points, whatever our wellness or illness, however much life we have left in us. Writing, as you carefully imply, connects us with the body, with each other, with the world.

By way of an ending to my own contribution, it seems relevant to refer to my 2013 residency at Swansea University College of Medicine as a way of considering the context of our work within the broader culture. The relationship between art and science was at the heart of my residency, which involved talking to staff members and researchers in this prestigious college. It was gratifying to see that many experts working there still saw the connection! I would like to quote briefly from the poems I produced as an outcome:

I pluck a green pen from Paulina's cup, it says:
   Meddyg Gorau Meddyg Enaid—
     The best doctor is a doctor for the soul!

The earliest doctors were poets, it
is said: *hoelan*
meaning "making whole,"
the poet being a doctor
for the soul, for *Soul.*

This understanding of "soul" is something I gathered from reading James Hillman (1990). I take it to signify the creative impulse that makes us human. The endeavor to bring and maintain the arts into scientific research is a vital thing.

the body being not just limbs & organs
but molecules,
where soul flutters.

"Smart missiles"—
not just drugs but poems.

I first got involved in the college when I attended a talk by an expert on narrative, Arthur Frank. It was something of an epiphany for me when I realized that practitioners in the worlds of medicine and social science have been working with stories, metaphors, meanings we call poetic. This work is struggling to integrate itself into mainstream medical practice in the United Kingdom; precious time is needed for reflection to take place in training and practice, by students and practitioners, not to mention patients. Creative writing can enrich our thinking, make our experience more meaningful. It enhances what we do and who we are; it can bring soul to life in our fragile, transient, astonishing bodies.

Surely part of the meaning of our work as writers in health and social care is to contribute our soulful practice to a renewed culture, where the science and the arts of "living well" are once again engaged. And Ty Newydd, I feel, should be recognized for facilitating this work outside the academy, where

16

people from all walks of life can gather. After all is said and done, we're all in this together.

References

British Psychological Society. 2011. Society statement on DSM-5. Accessed August 15, 2014. http://www.bps.org.uk/news/society-statement-dsm-5.

Davies, James. 2013. *Cracked: Why psychiatry is doing more harm than good.* London: Icon.

Department of Health. 2013. Improving quality of life for people with long term conditions. Accessed August 17, 2014. https://www.gov.uk/government/policies/improving-quality-of-life-for-people-with-long-term-conditions.

Field, Victoria. 2012. Slip free of that lamb's clothing for truly you are a lark. In *Words for wellbeing,* edited by Carol Ross. Penrith: Cumbria NHS Trust.

——. 2014. *Beginning to find joy again: Wise words for wellbeing evaluation.* Unpublished.

Frost, Robert. 1973. Fire and ice. In *Selected poems.* London: Penguin.

Hamilton, Fiona. 2011. Signals, lines, and reflections. In *Writing routes,* edited by Gillie Bolton et al. London: Jessica Kingsley.

Hartill, Graham. 1998. The web of words: Collaborative writing and mental health. In *The self on the page,* edited by C. Hunt and F. Sampson. London: Jessica Kingsley.

——. 2003. *Lifelines.* Ledbury: Ledbury Poetry Festival.

——. 2011. Jim—The equation. The Glasfryn Project. Accessed October 19, 2014. http://lyndondavies.co.uk/w/1355/graham-hartill-jim-the-equation-2/.

Hillman, James. 1990. *The essential James Hillman: A blue fire.* Edited by Thomas Moore. London: Routledge.

Killick, John. 1998. A matter of the life and death of the mind: Creative writing and dementia sufferers. In *The self on the page,* edited by C. Hunt and F. Sampson. London: Jessica Kingsley.

Mazza, Nicholas. 2003. *Poetry therapy: Theory and practice.* New York and Hove: Brunner-Routledge.

Pennebaker, James. 2004. *Writing to heal: A guided journal for recovering from trauma and emotional upheaval.* Oakland, CA: New Harbinger.

Rilke, Rainer Maria. 2012. *Letters to a young poet.* Start Publishing LLC. Kindle Edition.

Shuttle, Penelope. 2010. When happiness returns after a long absence. In *Sandgrain and hourglass.* Tarset, North Umbria: Bloodaxe.

2

Your Brain on Ink

Expressive Writing and Neuroplasticity

Deborah Ross

My experience is what I agree to attend to. Only those items I notice shape my mind.

—*William James, 1890*

The brain takes the shape the mind rests upon.

—*Rick Hanson, 2011*

These two ideas, articulated more than one hundred years apart, reflect what has come to be known as *experience-dependent* neuroplasticity—the actual way the brain can change through accumulated experience. What if there is also a *self-directed* neuroplasticity—a method of accelerating experience-dependent neurological change through expressive writing? What happens to the brain on ink?

A Short Course in Neuroplasticity

Neuroplasticity is the ability of the brain to change its structure in response to experience. That experience is often a mental process, such as perceiving, thinking, feeling, or remembering. It may be a process of focusing, sustaining, and shifting attention. It may be emotional, sensory, or imaginal in nature. The experience can be, and often is, a multimodal combination of two or more processes.

Neurons are the basic cells of the nervous system. Any time we are in the midst of experiencing, we are activating neurons. Any time a neuron is firing, its connection to other neurons (which occurs in the *synapses,* or the space between the neurons) is growing stronger (Siegel 2012).

We have two blueprints for how the brain engages in processing information as we move from the womb into infancy, childhood, and beyond. The first, experience-*expectant* connections, anticipates the basic sensory input that will be part of a child's world and has created synaptic connections that will enable that information to be processed. The second, experience-*dependent*, creates synaptic connections based on the actual experiences that we have as we engage with the world and the people that are part of it (Siegel 2012).

Before we are born and as infants, our genes have set up experience-expectant connections. When we, as infants, receive basic sensory input such as light, sound, or scent, the brain must translate that input into actually seeing, hearing, or smelling. This is true for all of the senses. The human brain has been encoded to anticipate these sensory experiences, and the genes have set up the corresponding synaptic connections that are the perceptual systems known as sight, hearing, taste, touch, and smell.

Taking it further, we also have a mechanism to foster experience-dependent connections that are created by the very experiences that we have as our lives unfold. Our individual worlds are full of sights, sounds, scents, tastes, and touch, each of which comes with particular and unique associations and meanings: the food served in our homes, the sounds accompanying meals, and the people with whom we share our meals. Those experiences activate the genes that create the synaptic connections that are unique to the meanings that are created with those experiences.

Glossary and Guide to Your Brain

Amygdala: The brain's alarm bell. Centrally located in the limbic region, it's involved in the activation of emotion, processing of social signals, and the appraisal of meaning.

Attention: The process that regulates the flow of information. We can aim it, sustain it, or shift it

Brain: Often refers to the skull or "head brain," but can mean the extended nervous system in the body that includes the neural processors around the heart and gut.

Hippocampus: Centrally located in the limbic region, it plays a major role in memory and gives the brain a sense of the self in time and space.

Memory: *Explicit* requires focused attention and is factual/autobiographic: recalling the bike ride that you took last week. *Implicit* does not require focused attention and can include perceptions, emotions, bodily sensations: riding the bike itself.

Name it to tame it: The finding that placing a label on an experience can calm the mind and stabilize attention.

Neural Darwinism: "Use it or lose it; survival of the busiest." Neural connections that aren't used are pruned or wither away.

Neurons that fire together wire together: Donald Hebb's proposal that neurons that happened to fire together once will likely fire together in the future because synaptic linkages were created during the first firing. Freud proposed essentially the same thing in his Law of Association when he said that events experienced together will be associated with each other in memory.

Neuroplasticity: The ability of the brain to change itself in response to attention and experience. How you use your mind or focus your attention changes your brain.

Velcro/Teflon Negativity Bias: The brain is like Velcro for negative experiences and Teflon for positive. Survival messages stick and positive quality of life messages need conscious cultivation.

From Freud to FMRIs

Much of the research on neuroplasticity in recent decades parallels the development of new technologies, specifically Functional Magnetic Resonance Imaging (FMRI), which detects changes in blood flow in the brain. When a region of the brain is occupied or engaged, blood flow to that region increases and we can now see and measure actual circulatory brain changes; we can observe the activity of neurons and synapses and how they connect, interact, and strengthen.

However, even though the technology that enables us to track these changes is modern, neuroplasticity was actually described in the nineteenth century by Sigmund Freud. In 1888 Freud proposed his Law of Association by Simultaneity, which hypothesized that when two neurons fire simultaneously, an ongoing association between the two is created. The psychoanalytic concept of "free association," in which a patient is asked to recall everything that comes to mind, no matter how random, trivial, or seemingly irrelevant and unrelated, is actually an expression of the linkages that Freud believed had been created in our memory networks (Amacher 1965). Might these linkages be the brain maps that became the object of study more than a half-century later?

In the 1930s, the inquiry moved across the Atlantic from Europe to North America. Montreal neurosurgeon Dr. Wilder Penfield, while performing surgery on cancer and epilepsy patients, began to explore this question of whether brain maps actually exist. Because there are no pain receptors in the brain itself, patients can be conscious during brain surgery, which yields a collaborative experience between patient and doctor. By stimulating different parts of the cerebral cortex, Penfield was able to accomplish two things: He was able to make sure that during surgery he was not removing healthy tissue along with diseased tissue, and patients were able to participate in the mapping of both the sensory and motor areas of the brain. This resulted in the unusual discovery that areas that are next to one another on the body's surface are also usually next to one another on the brain maps (Penfield and Rasmussen 1950).

In addition, Penfield noticed that when he touched certain parts of the brain with his probe, childhood memories returned. This discovery might have suggested that mental activities also are mapped in the brain. At the time, however, prevailing scientific thought assumed that these maps were not only fixed and unchanging, but universal. The mistaken belief was that humans, regardless of unique histories, circumstances, and stories of meaning that were created, all displayed the same mapping sequence. Now, of course, we know that the concept of "one brain fits all" is simply not true (Kandel 2006).

It wasn't until the end of the next decade, in 1949, that psychologist Donald Hebb began to shift this concept by proposing that when one neuron fires and thus causes another to fire sequentially, or when two neurons fire at the same time repeatedly, chemical changes will occur in both neurons, resulting in a stronger connection between the two. Thus, Hebb suggested, the very structure of a neuron can be altered by experience. As the sum total of our experiences is unique to us as individuals, so, too, is the map that corresponds to those experiences (Hebb 1949).

Another way to think about that concept is that a map of New York City does not look like a map of Bismarck, North Dakota, even as we recognize that both are maps, and both can be drawn utilizing the same set of symbols to describe the terrain. These cities grew up around the unique needs of their inhabitants, and our brains model the unique structures created by their hosts.

Forty years later, by the late 1980s, Michael Merzenich had become one of the leading researchers of brain maps. We now had a new way of talking about these researchers and practitioners: they were called neuroplasticians. One of the questions that occupied Merzenich was whether brain maps are created and could then be modified by manipulating the timing of the input to them. He demonstrated in multiple elegantly designed experiments that neurons that fired together in time wired together to make a map that could then be modified according to how often that circuit fired (Merzenich et al. 1984).

Neurobiologist Carla Shatz (1992) coined the phrase "neurons that fire together wire together" that neatly sums up the findings from these researchers of the late twentieth century. Further research from Robert Post and others have added "and survive together" (Post and Weiss 1997). Just as our physical fitness follows the "use it or lose it," model, so does our brain. Neurons that have fired together repeatedly are less likely to be lost to disuse and the brain's ability to prune "dead wood." Conversely, areas that are repeatedly and consistently used can thicken and grow strong, as was demonstrated by the scans of the brains of London taxi drivers who, before being granted a license to operate a taxi, undergo an extensive two-year training that involves memorizing an intricate array of London streets and landmarks (Maguire et al. 2000). Another way to describe this phenomenon might be as neural Darwinism, or "survival of the busiest (brain circuits)."

The Brain as Velcro and Teflon

As this research has continued, other aspects of neuroplasticity have become known that can help us understand how expressive writing strategies may be developed in the service of healing, growth, and integration.

The first is an understanding that the brain actually has a default position: we are wired to embrace negativity. Our brains are "Velcro for the negative and Teflon for the positive" (Hanson 2013). Why does it make sense to have our brains, like a powerful vacuum cleaner in our skull, scanning for, sweeping in, and fiercely holding onto the negative?

Neuroscientist Jaak Panksepp (1998) suggests that our brain represents a kind of living museum. It contains all of our cavemen/women ancestors, beginning with Neanderthals, through Cro-Magnons, along with ancient versions of all of the creatures from the sea to the land—jellyfish to lizards to gorillas. In those times where survival, not quality of life, was the order of the day, the operative question was not, "What am I going to have for lunch?" but rather, "Am I going to be lunch?"

Our evolutionary history, encoded in our brains, primes us to learn as quickly as possible from bad experiences. Those learnings ride an express track into the brain's storage centers; we are set up to learn much faster from pain than pleasure:

- Couples therapist John Gottman (1994, 1999) reports that in healthy marriages a ratio of five positive comments to each negative keeps the marital eco-system robust (1994). He also suggests dedicated blocks of time—no multitasking!—that are devoted to admiration, appreciation, and affection. It is vital that we take in the good (1999). It is common for couples to struggle with how to offer a fully positive appreciation for their partner or take in a fully positive expression of love and caring.

- We tend to live in a zone where we are more inclined to language something in the negative—all that we *do not* want or *are not* receiving. Even positive expressions are often weak and merely reflect the absence of the negative. Progress in therapy, for instance, is often expressed as, "*I'm not as* stressed/anxious/depressed today."
- Should we be offered a lovely gift of gratitude or praise, we often hiccup or deflect rather than embrace the gift by fully taking it in. "Yes, but," is the phrase that often drives our relationships with others as well as the one we have with ourselves. We respond like nonstick Teflon for the good that comes to us.

Our evolutionary, ancestral wiring has rendered us highly skilled at learning bad lessons from bad experiences and has left us rank amateurs at learning the good lessons from positive experiences. In addition, our radar for the negative also contributes to how we store not only the memories of an experience but the translation of these experiences into expectations, assumptions, overall beliefs about ourselves and others, including a sense of who is "other" in our world. In the end, we have an imbalance in favor of the negative, which was useful for survival under harsh and threatening conditions. That imbalance includes both an internal radar sweep for impending negative experiences, an *amygdala* that sets off its own alarm bells with attention-getting urgency, and a rapid encoding of those experiences in our brain. We go from negative mental state to negative neural trait with dazzling efficiency.

The Brain Enjoys Novelty

So, how do we use all of this information about how the brain is primed to ensure that we survive, but is rather uninterested in whether we thrive? How do we create a more Velcro-like experience for the positive? What is helpful? How does expressive writing help construct a lasting story with headlines that are encouraging, healing, and reflect a vision of the kind of life we wish to lead?

First things first: we must intentionally engage in an installation process. We must take in or internalize the positive so that we can turn positive mental states into positive neural traits.

In the service of that installation, we turn to another key finding, that the brain enjoys novelty. In at least one area of our brain, the *hippocampus*, which has a significant role in appraising and consolidating information from short-term to long-term memory, novelty helps that process. The hippocampus is also quite vulnerable to the stress hormone *cortisol*. Neurons can be weakened or killed in the presence of cortisol, particularly if it is part of the daily soup served in the brain. That toxic meal will actually shrink the hippocampus itself.

However, the hippocampus is also a primary site where neurons are born, and their survival odds are enhanced by the presence of novel experiences. When we are playful, spontaneous, and inviting new experiences or new ways of noticing our experience, we encourage the brain to grow (Hanson 2013).

The well-being of the hippocampus makes it more likely that the alarm bell sounded by the adjacent amygdala will be appropriately evaluated and perhaps modulated.[1] The amygdala's job as fire alarm for our system is to get us to "act before we think," and the hippocampus, when it is healthy, is able to use memory to question whether this level of urgency is really appropriate for the situation. A key role for the hippocampus is, therefore, its ability to assess the context in which the alarm is screeching.

Findings from the research on posttraumatic stress disorder (PTSD) suggest that those suffering from PTSD have a smaller hippocampus. This is a complex finding because we do not yet know whether someone is more likely to suffer from PTSD *because* they have a smaller hippocampus or whether the stressors that led to PTSD are the result of the shrinkage of the hippocampus. Perhaps it is both. Regardless, encouraging the growth of the hippocampus is one avenue to consider as we encourage the resolution of the posttraumatic stress (*Science Daily* 2011).

When our neurons are firing, and all circuits involved in the activity are a "go," then the genes in those cells are primed to become more active. That activity can invite two processes, one that yields better synaptic connections between neurons, making communication more efficient, and one that can increase the insulation around the axon, or the tail of the neuron. Increased insulation makes it possible for the neuron to work so efficiently that its functioning can improve as much as 3000 percent because impulses travel much faster. In addition, the recovery time of the nerve is shortened so it can fire again after a shorter rest period (Siegel 2012).

These neural findings eminently support the importance of *practice, practice, practice.* Those who have been recognized for their achievements in music, art, athletics, undoubtedly have beautifully insulated nerve axons in the regions of the brain that mediate their unique skills.

Practice can also refer to having a practice that is in service of the skill of well being. Richie Davidson, founder and director of the Center for Investigating Healthy Minds at the University of Wisconsin–Madison, has spent years studying how our brains change in response to how we focus our attention. Beginning in 1992, when he started studying the brains of the Dalai Lama and his Tibetan monks, and continuing to the present time, Davidson has been working to understand how mindfulness-based practices can contribute to our well-being, noting how our brains change in the process cultivating these practices (Davidson and Begley 2012).

Having a regular journal-writing practice, which is a concrete and verifiable form of attention, shares common features with mindfulness-based meditation practices. Even when we sit down and free-write with no particular focus or direction, we were intentional about choosing the activity. In picking up our journal and pen or opening the screen of our digital journal, a choice was made to engage our brain in this activity.

There are many writing exercises that invite us to direct and focus our attention in very specific ways. Responding to any journal prompt invites attention and focus on that prompt. An additional step that seems to bring journaling even more in line with mindfulness-based meditation practices is reflecting on the completed write and the process of doing it. When we are present to what emerges on the page by reading what we have just written and writing a few sentences about what we noticed, we are developing an observational part of our brain. We are gaining separation from the write itself and taking note of both the process of writing and any insights that the writing yielded. What happened in my body as I wrote? Did my handwriting change? Was there a smile on my face or tears in my eyes? Were there any "aha" moments? (Adams 2013). Paying attention, cultivating curiosity, and noticing what emerges as a function of the process of writing can be seen as similar to meditation practices that cultivate concentration and invite insight.

Thus, we see a direct line from the theoretical conceptualizations of Freud, who proposed his version of a mind map known as the Law of Association, to the classic psychoanalytic technique of free association, to the research of Hebb in the 1940s that suggested that neurons that fire together wire together. This leads to the notion that these circuits either survive together as a function of their higher rates of utilization or, if not regularly fired, will likely be pruned out of the system through early adulthood, then wither. We have the building blocks to understand the powerful research findings that link neuroplasticity to attention and how we use our minds. Whether we show up and pay attention, how we direct that attention, whether it is focused or diffuse, whether it includes novelty and enrichment—all of these choices, repeated consistently over time, will actually change the shape of our brain.

These changes are bivalent; if we focus on the negative, ruminate over losses, and attend to our betrayals and slights, we will have a brain that is reflective of the structures necessary to support those thoughts and emotions. Multitasking or living in a zone of distraction rather than focusing on the person who is in front of us at this moment, or the task at hand, does not support the release of neurotransmitters that invite positive brain change. But if we are focused in our attention, intentional about noticing the positive in our life; when we are playful, spontaneous, and generous with introducing novelty; when we tune in rather than out, we invite the growth of neural circuits that have significantly integrative, healing properties.

Becoming a Journaling Neuroplastician: Case Studies

How do we bring all of this scientific research to the process of becoming journaling neuroplasticians? How can all of these concepts be taught to our clients so that they might use their written words in service of their healing, growth, greater well-being, happiness, and a deeper sense of personal integration? To begin, let's revisit a children's classic, the story of Harold and his purple crayon.

Written in 1955, Crockett Johnson's book, *Harold and the Purple Crayon*, is the story of a little boy, Harold, who drew his way into a grand magical adventure. The work has elements of fantastical, imaginative wanderings. Harold also drew landmarks to ensure that he could find his way home and resources that he could "draw" on if he got into difficulty.

Often considered an example of an art book, it is a story constructed for adventure and magical journey. It reminds us that our minds can create a new story, where we are excited, challenged, and resourced to live a life that makes us proud to be its author. We may not be writing with a purple crayon, nor may we be relying on our drawing skills as Harold did, but with our journal and a set of expressive writing skills we can author a healing tale in service of a well-lived life that has adventure, connection, integrity, and a sense of fulfillment. That is what three of my therapy clients, Dorothy, Jack, and Bert,[2] might tell you. Here are their stories.

When therapy-savvy Dorothy first came into my office, she was distressed that she was still falling back into telling herself the same tired story, leading to the same habituated outcomes and a sense of resignation about her life. Knowing that I am trained in journal therapy, she hoped to gain some relief by exploring her relationship with her story via a notebook and pen. She was also specifically drawn to journal writing as it affords a readily available, portable, accessible form of healing. Originally likened to a "first aid kit" for her soul, her journal became a reservoir of healing possibilities.

Meanwhile, another new client, Jack, described himself as a "neck-up kind of guy." Jack wondered whether writing might help him explore his feelings. Recognized for his accomplishments and well regarded within his field, he approached the relationships in his life as problems to be solved. He often found himself puzzled about why the solutions he offered, that seemed so obvious to him on the "spreadsheet of life," were not readily embraced by his family and close friends or associates. Indeed, to his bewilderment, they were sometimes a source of further irritation or alienation. A health scare brought him into my office. He was unfamiliar with vulnerability, and when he suddenly began welling up with tears during poignant scenes in movies, he called for an intake appointment.

Bert arrived in the United States as a child, his family having fled their war-torn home country. He began writing poetry and song lyrics as a teenager, occasionally dabbling in a journal, but he kept that activity under wraps—that was something his sisters did. Noticing that sharing poems or songs could bring something transformative to his close relationships, he was interested in exploring the more personal dimensions of the written word. Might writing transform him? He had stumbled onto a career path via a recruiter at a college job fair. While this path likely would afford sufficient financial compensation to support a family and was seen as a safe and secure occupation that honored his parent's wishes, he was wondering what happened to those parts of himself that had been enchanted by playing with words. "Who am I?" he asked.

Part of my work with clients includes an education about the brain, the current findings in neuroscience, and the hopeful messages embedded in the concept of self-directed neuroplasticity. Because I am also credentialed as a journal therapist, and I believe in the power of writing to accelerate self-directed neuroplasticity, I give my clients journal assignments. A first step is to get a baseline write.

I ask clients to do Cluster diagrams (Adams 1990) of their brains. We start with a blank sheet of paper. In the middle of the page the client writes the words "My brain," or perhaps his own first name: "Jack's brain" or "Bert's brain." Then the client is invited to explore all of the associations that he has with his brain. Lines connect circles that create a visual map of associations, physical characteristics, mysteries, challenges, and competencies. The relationships between these aspects are manifested in the web-like drawing that has organically emerged. Additional clusters can be created along the way so that there is a pictorial representation of the evolution of new maps.

The cluster technique is also on a lower rung of the Journal Ladder (Adams 1998) and therefore is a more structured, stable, contained write that yields information as well as some insight and awareness of patterns. It is a good choice for someone who is just beginning to engage in the process of expressive writing and perhaps is feeling a little unsteady. Dorothy was encouraged that we had another way to "look" at her story. Jack recognized the cluster from the business world (where he called it "mind mapping"), and that helped him feel more at home in the writing process. Bert, who had learned about some of neuroscience findings in a psychology class, just thought what we were doing was "cool!"

Another option that I offer in alignment with conversation about self-directed neuroplasticity is a three-part Sentence Stem:

My mind usually rests upon _____. Filled with _____, I imagine that my brain looks like _____.

This is often the first time that a client has considered the relationship that they have with their brain. Jack saw himself in a new light when he wrote:

My mind usually rests upon flow charts. Filled with intersecting lines, I imagine that my brain looks like a power grid.

I always teach my clients about the reflection write process (Adams 2013). It is the key to developing the observational muscle necessary to notice what is happening as a function of writing. At the conclusion of the write, the client is asked to read it and write two or three sentences about both the write itself and the process of writing. What does she notice? What is she aware of? Were there any surprises or "aha" moments? In addition, my clients are invited to track the embodied physicality of the writing process itself. Did his handwriting change? Did he notice himself gripping the pen? Was he relaxed and feeling confident, or did he notice places in his body that were holding tension? For Jack, being focused on the embodiment of the process was a key to helping him develop "below the neck" awareness so that he could begin to name those feelings that were now bubbling up.

While our minds can be scanning or projecting into the future or reviewing/ruminating about the past, it is our bodies that are in real time. Tracking the embodied experience of writing helps to keep clients grounded in the present moment. There is growing evidence that resolution of trauma needs to involve the body, so checking in with the embodied experience of writing is a good gauge of how a client's nervous system is processing the writing. Developing this observational muscle via the reflection write seems akin to the noticing that happens when we engage in mindfulness-based meditation practice.

Dorothy, Jack, and Bert did all of their journaling by hand, as do most of my clients. Those who write on-screen may sacrifice clues that handwriting reveals, but the core reflection process is equally applicable to handwriting or digital writing. Sometimes the client feels disappointment that the write did not yield as much as was hoped for, and that is noted, too. All observations are welcome.

After reviewing her cluster, Dorothy reflected on the many negative threads that were the source of rumination in her brain. She had a self-described failed marriage and had dropped out of college to marry, thereby letting go of a career path that actually required an advanced degree. She noted artistry, creativity, and some good problem-solving skills, but they were a smaller part of her brain. Where her brain habitually rested was on her perceived shortcomings. For example, she worried that a section of her brain had been damaged by the drinking that she had done as a teen.

Jack's cluster revealed that much of his brain was devoted to thinking and problem solving. There was a space devoted to his internal dictionary, and right beside it was his pride at his facility with language. Although his brain did rest on the relationships in his life, they were further away—more remote, as was a more heart-centered vocabulary.

In his reflection, Bert's brain sizzled and crackled with possibilities, side by side with his concerns about how many of them would be realized. He noticed that the circuitry related to his family was strong, as was a sense of possibility. He wanted to have a stronger link between possibility and purpose. That would become a key circuit in our work together.

Taking in the Good

I always explain to my clients about the Velcro/Teflon model for negative and positive experiences. It helps to normalize the brain's bias toward skewed storage of negative experience and worldviews so that, rather than chastise themselves or engage in any more relentless self-improvement projects, clients can appreciate how their wiring was installed in service of keeping them alive. It is an ancestral connection that accomplished its mission (we are sitting and breathing together), and I encourage clients to honor it with gratitude.

However, the question remains of how to open up to positive experiences so that our brain maps contain that location. Hanson (2011) refers to it as "taking in the good." These experiences, which often pass unnoticed, have the potential to become sources of strength or resilience. They must be installed in order to become a resource; installation is a deliberate multipronged process.

Writing is both an accelerant to the brain remapping and a handy tool for installation. I use Hanson's HEAL model to craft writing suggestions:

- Have a positive experience and hold it
- Enrich it
- Absorb it
- Link the positive to associated negative material (Hanson 2013) This final step nudges the negative out of its McMansion-like space in the brain into a more appropriate downsized version.

To help address Dorothy's propensity for rumination, and to engage her journal as a partner in the installation of the positive process, I suggested that Dorothy complete a Captured Moment—a brief story about a time of intense sensory engagement (Adams 1990). She was asked either to notice something positive in the moment, or recall a positive experience. Sometimes clients can sense the presence of something positive that has not yet emerged but can focus on it and bring it forward to the page. It is important to saturate the write with as much sensory memory as possible. These writes benefit from some guided imagery to invite the experience into the foreground and are followed with a reflection write.

Dorothy had strong positive memories of times with her grandmother, whom she described as a "woman ahead of her time." She wrote about her grandmother's resilience and self-determination. That led to her noticing the ways in which she had felt the flush of pride in her own resourcefulness. One can see the beginnings of linkage of circuits, how noticing one thing leads to noticing something else. Neurons that are "firing together" are "wiring together."

In between our sessions I encouraged Dorothy to practice noticing the positive and then writing a captured moment. This encourages both the installation and the cultivation of writing as a practice through experiencing the prompts that are ever-present in the world and reaching for a pen to engage with them.

In subsequent sessions she reported recall of some positive memories as well as awareness of a positive element of a difficult situation and some generally positive moments in the day, the kind of moments that previously would have been missed or dismissed. As she got more comfortable with this form of writing, it was time to move to the second step—enriching it.

Enrichment and Absorption

Five factors, identified from the research on the neuropsychology of learning, are brought into the *enrichment* step: *duration, intensity, multimodality, novelty,* and *personal relevance.*

All five factors are explained prior to the actual write.

Our negative states make their way into our memory banks on a dedicated express track. The positive ones, however, ride the local. To install a positive experience, therefore, we must pay attention to holding it in the foreground of our memory for at least five seconds. (Ten is better, and twenty seconds is optimal.) That does not sound like a long time, but our minds are easily distracted. Twenty seconds of focusing on a positive memory can feel like forever to one who has not yet cultivated mindfulness skills. I encourage clients to reach for the goal of twenty seconds, and I assure them that any amount will yield a dividend.

As the memory or experience is held, honoring the *duration* portion of the installation process, we turn to the second factor, *intensity,* which can partner with the third, *multimodality.* Allowing the experience to be as intense as possible and saturating it with awareness from multiple sources is next. What is the entire sensory/bodily experience of this memory? What are the emotions associated with the experience?

To help with recall, an additional element can be introduced. Smell is the most primitive of the five senses. Therefore, I sometimes suggest that these captured moments be paired with a personally meaningful scent, even if this scent has nothing directly to do with this particular memory. Dorothy's grandmother wore a particular cologne, and Dorothy was able to approximate its primary notes through a mixture of essential oils. She reported that it seemed to help deepen the recall experience, particularly when practiced over time.

Novelty, or what is unusual in this experience either in a larger way or in more of a tickling, is the next factor. Bert found that he was more easily able to juxtapose his creative dreams and his doubts and fears when he turned his notebook ninety degrees and wrote sideways across the page. I keep colorful pens and stickers available for my clients to help them add some *novelty* to their writing.

The last factor is *personal relevance*. What does this positive experience have to do with the self? Why does it matter? How might it be helpful or supportive to take in this experience? As Jack practiced tenderness and caring with his wife and children and held the memory of intimacy for increasingly more seconds at a time, he began to develop a richer understanding of vulnerability.

Hanson describes this enrichment process as similar to gathering wood, lighting a fire, adding logs that will burn longer than the kindling, and then taking in the warmth. Dorothy and others report that incorporating these principles into the writing process can produce a kind of inner glow, often subtle, more ember-like at first but, with practice, an inner warmth that feels more sustaining.

Dorothy, Jack, and Bert all used multimodal strategies to help with the *absorption* stage. Because the brain likes novelty, and activation of the senses is important for *enrichment* and *absorption*, I invited all of them to consider how they might bring an additional dimension to their writing. Sometimes they opened a window if the weather was suitable and felt the breeze, heard the birds, or noticed outdoor scents. Dorothy preferred silence. Jack and Bert gravitated toward music, although they made very different choices, and they primed their writes by listening to or playing a piece of music that they associated with the memory or experience that they were going to recall. Like Proust's madeleine, which led to the multivolume *Remembrance of Things Past*, sometimes food was involved as an additional writing cue.

Linking to the Positive

Before we reach the final stage of HEAL, softening the negative by *linking* it to the positive, it is common for parts of ourselves that are skeptical of all this emphasis on the positive to announce themselves. Because of my training in "parts work," notably the Internal Family Systems model of therapy, I normalize their presence, their protective messages, and how it makes sense that they would be keepers of the skepticism.

In terms of journal writes, it often makes sense at this point to invite a dialogue (a written conversation where the client writes both parts from shifted perspectives, somewhat similar to the Gestalt empty-chair process) with a part of the client's system that is skeptical—sometimes downright hostile—to this newfangled positive way of being. Allowing the concerns to emerge on the page or in session makes it much less likely that the "inner skeptics" will deepen an underground fault line. Dorothy's dialogue revealed some childhood messages that had to do with a list of "don'ts," all of which reinforced a core message about the importance of "staying under the radar" and following a narrow path. Making noise, being exuberant, lifting her head to smell the roses (and enjoy the scent!) were frowned upon.

Even as skeptical parts are likely to show up again, and will be ripe for more processing and more dialogues, we can still move into the linkage of positive to negative by bringing into the room a negative experience. I invite clients to pick a recent negative experience, one that was challenging but not traumatic. Dorothy picked a difficult interaction with a coworker. The linkage process begins with inviting a positive association—in Dorothy's case, to recall her grandmother's assertiveness—to move into the foreground, while the negative is shifted to the background, and the positive is *held*, *enriched*, and *absorbed* following the guidelines. This process invites a conscious, written association of positive with negative so that when the event is returned to memory, it will go with the positive associations.

As Dorothy did this exercise and gained greater facility in moving the negative to the background and the positive to the foreground, she then anchored the experience by writing. On reflection she noticed that she was actually more skilled in being clear about her boundaries than she had given herself credit for. She could see that she had sidestepped potentially escalating areas of the conversation by refusing to engage.

For Jack and Bert the HEAL process was similar, but with an additional piece. Sometimes I invite clients to set a theme or intention as we begin our work together. It emerges from the first "My Brain" cluster and reflection write. For the intention I introduce the AlphaPoem (Adams 1998).

The alphapoem begins with writing, vertically in a column down the left side of the page, the letters of a word or short phrase that is emerging as a theme. Then a poem is written, line by line, with each successive line starting with a word that begins with the predetermined letter. Clients heed instructions to "write quickly, and don't think too much," and poems emerge in three minutes or less.

The alphapoem initially was a mixed experience for Jack. He liked the idea of inviting words that were arranged in a familiar column format, but he struggled to come up with a theme or intention. He tried out several along the way, using his developing sense of the poetic to decide whether he was on the right track. As the words "love" or "heart" started to show up for the alphapoem, he was able to notice or recall experiences that manifested those qualities—from memories of childhood pets to newly created memories of his grandchildren. These memories started to form the basis of the captured moments that he wrote about using the HEAL protocol.

Alpha Poem on Integrity

I nstead of

N egativity, I place my

T houghts and actions in

E nergizing the

G oodness that surrounds me—

R eally all the time if

I just pay attention and

T rust that I know when to

Y ield to my own better nature.

Bert was excited to create a poem and appreciative of an invitation to bring that into our work. Then, as he looked at his cluster, he found himself drawing a blank about the word or phrase that would represent the theme for our work. I suggested several, including *courage*, because he had wondered aloud if he had the courage to "live bolder" than the family messages. I mentioned *integration*, because he talked about his many parts and how they might be manifested in an integrated whole. His catch phrase became "Can I put ketchup on this?" a reference to division that existed in his world of food, too. From Bert I realized, again, that the acronym, WAIT (Why Am I Talking) is a pillar in the world of journaling as well as therapy. My suggested word is not likely to ever be as powerful or colorful a match as the one that my clients come up with. In Bert's case the word was *kaleidoscope*.

Once Bert had his word he used his Captured Moment writes, following the HEAL protocol, to notice facets, how they came together to make one colorful whole, how they shifted, and how they represented *integrity*, a word that later became his theme.

Dorothy was intrigued by the shifts she was making. Her next cluster about her brain showed growing resources. With a shy smile and more respect for her ability to make these shifts, she decided to go back to college, finish her degree, and open some doors to a new career path. Now her story about herself has a comma rather than a period as more possibilities emerge. Although she didn't want to do an alphapoem at the beginning of our work together, she did come back to it, not particularly to set an intention but as a way of creating new chapter headings in her story.

Jack, while initially drawn to the cluster because it was so familiar from the business world, noticed that he became more intrigued with other ways of writing as he became more aware of his feelings, connections, and relationships. He did return to the "My Brain" cluster, however; he was surprised to learn that, as he considers retirement, his brain is resting on the relationships that were formed over the course of his work. His awards and accolades are still important, but they have receded in prominence. His mind has stretched into greater flexibility, and he joked that he just might create a relationship spreadsheet where he could appreciate the qualities of the people in his life— the birth of a new journal technique!

Bert's later cluster showed the "snap, crackle, and pop" that he loves experiencing, but there was more linkage and circuitry as he found outlets for his writing. Even as he continues on his career path, he is blogging and going to "open mic" nights at a local poetry venue that is drawing a younger crowd, many of whom are immigrants. He is still grappling with questions related to his identity, but he is doing more of it in a community that supports the written and spoken word as a lifeline. He noticed that his customary seriousness had developed a spur circuit—humor.

Although simplified here, there is a toggling process that occurs in the sessions and the writing, guided by two questions: *Where is my mind resting?* and *How might I invite it to rest in a place where I am cultivating the qualities that support me living an integrated, sustainable, joyful life?* The journal prompts tend to emerge organically from the cultivation of these questions and the places where our clients feel stuck.

Conclusion

Our brains change, and it is not in our best interest to have them change quickly. Imagine the chaos of installing a new operating system on your computer each night. There are, though, some practices that open the channels for change. We already know from decades of research that as few as three days of structured writing can promote health and emotional well-being. A long-term practice of writing for neurological change may be an entrance ramp for the development of neural pathways, just as mindfulness practices have shown to be. When we encourage our clients to reach for their pens, we may be helping them spell *neuroplasticity* in a life well lived.

References

Adams, Kathleen. 1990. *Journal to the self: Twenty-two paths to personal growth.* New York: Warner Books.

———. 1998. *The way of the journal: A journal therapy workbook for healing.* 2nd ed. Lutherville, MD: Sidran Press.

———. 2013. Expression and reflection: Toward a new paradigm in expressive writing. In *Expressive writing: Foundations of practice*, edited by K. Adams. Lanham, MD: Rowman & Littlefield Education, 1–29.

Amacher, Peter. 1965. *Freud's neurological education and its influence on psychoanalytic theory.* New York: International Universities Press.

Davidson, Richard, and Sharon Begley. 2012. *The emotional life of your brain.* New York: Hudson Street Press.

Gottman, John. 1994. *Why marriages succeed or fail.* New York: Simon and Schuster.

———. 1999. *The seven principles for making marriage work.* New York: Three Rivers Press.

Hanson, Rick. 2011. *Just one thing.* Oakland, CA: New Harbinger Publications.

———. 2013. *Hardwiring happiness.* New York: Crown.

Hebb, Donald. 1949. *The organization of behavior: A neuropsychological theory.* Hoboken, NJ: John Wiley & Sons.

James, William. 1890 (reprinted 2013). *The principles of psychology.* Vol. 1. New York: Cosimo Classics.

Johnson, Crockett. 1955. *Harold and the purple crayon.* New York: Harper and Row.

Kandel, Eric. 2006. *In search of memory: The emergence of a new science of mind.* New York: Norton.

Maguire, E., D. Gadian, I. Johnrusde, C. Good, J. Ashburner, R. Frackowiak, and C. Frith. 2000. Navigation-related structural change in the hippocampi of taxi drivers. *Proceedings of the National Academy of Sciences* 97: 4398–403.

Merzenich, M., R. Nelson, M. Stryker, M. Cynader, A. Schoppmann, and J. Zook. 1984. Somatosensory cortical map changes following digit amputation in adult monkeys. *Journal of Comparative Neurology* 224(4):591–605.

Panksepp, Jaak. 1998. *Affective neuroscience: The foundations of human and animal emotions.* Oxford: Oxford University Press.

Panksepp, Jaak, and L. Biven. 2012. *The archeology of mind: Neuroevolutionary origins of human emotions.* New York: Norton.

Penfield, Wilder, and Theodore Rasmussen. 1950. *The cerebral cortex of man.* New York: Macmillan.

Post, R. M., and S. R. B. Weiss. 1997. Emergent properties of neural systems: How focal molecular neurobiological alterations can affect behavior. *Development and Psychopathology* 10:829–56.

Science Daily. 2011. Hippocampal volume and resilience in postraumatic stress disorder. March 23.

Shatz, Carla. 1992. The developing brain. *Scientific American* 267(3):60–67.

Siegel, Daniel J. 2012. *The pocket guide to interpersonal neurobiology.* New York: Norton.

Notes

1. It should be noted that although it is common to refer to both the amygdala and the hippocampus in the singular, as if we have only one of each, in fact we have two of each. Both the right and left temporal lobes of our brain have an amygdala and a hippocampus.

2. Fictionalized names for composited clients.

3

Expressive Writing for Caregiver Resilience

A Research Perspective

John F. Evans, Meredith Mealer, Karen Jooste, and Marc Moss

The writing is very enlightening. This week I found myself writing facts at first and then realizing how I was really feeling about the situation. I was able to step back and really focus on what was actually my challenge. The challenge was not what I actually thought. The writing helped me to realize the real feelings and emotions about what was going on. I was then able to find some solutions to my challenge and how to make it and me better. It is nice to stop and take a minute to really see how I am feeling. It helps put things in perspective.

– *Study participant*

In this chapter, we describe a twelve-week expressive writing intervention implemented from January to April 2013 with ICU nurses. This writing intervention was part of a pilot program of multimodal practices to build ICU nurse resilience under the direction of Meredith Mealer and Marc Moss, Chief of the Critical Care and Pulmonary Units at the University of Colorado Hospital in Denver/Aurora. Here we provide the background, methodology, results, and pilot study conclusions and describe the one-day expressive writing workshop and the twelve weeks of follow-up writing. We end with recommendations for further study.

Background

Critical care nurses work in a stressful environment and are often challenged by the tension-charged environment that exposes them to high patient mortality and morbidity and daily ethical dilemmas, including addressing end-of-life issues and prolonging life in futile situations. As a consequence, cumulative exposure to indirect traumatic experiences increases the risk of developing common psychological disorders when working as a bedside ICU nurse. It has been reported that ICU nurses in the United States have a high prevalence of posttraumatic stress disorder (PTSD), burnout syndrome (BOS), anxiety, and depression (Mealer, Burnham et al. 2009).

In an environment with such a high degree of stress and the possibility of physical and emotional harm to caregivers, resilience is a crucial attribute. We define resilience as a psychological construct that includes personal qualities that enable one to thrive in the face of adversity. Resilience can be learned and is considered one of the most important factors when assessing adjustment following trauma. Recent evidence (Mealer, Jones et al. 2012) suggests that ICU nurses who are resilient and practice resilient coping mechanisms are better able to adapt to the stressful ICU work environment. Highly resilient ICU nurses are significantly less likely to develop PTSD, BOS, anxiety, and depression compared to ICU nurses who are not resilient. Additionally, highly resilient ICU nurses are less likely to report difficulty functioning outside of work in relationships and report higher overall life satisfaction compared with nonresilient ICU nurses (Mealer, Jones et al. 2012). However, resilience training in this population of healthcare providers is relatively unexplored. Therefore, we conducted a twelve-week randomized, controlled, multimodal resilience-training program for ICU nurses to determine if the program was feasible and acceptable.

One component of the resilience-training program consisted of expressive writing or written exposure therapy. This is a form of emotional writing that promotes cognitive processing and challenges distorted memories associated with traumatic events. This method was chosen because writing about traumatic and stressful events has been associated with improved physical and psychological health. Additionally, it has been reported (Smyth et al. 2008) that written disclosure significantly reduces PTSD symptom severity among traumatized groups. Expressive writing in ICU nurses is unexplored and may provide insight related to the emotional upheaval experienced as a result of work-related traumatic events. Also, it would allow our writing experts the opportunity to provide feedback using motivational interviewing techniques aimed at bolstering resilient cognitive strategies.

Methodology

The study recruited participants from a single academic institution. ICU nurses were eligible to participate in this study if they worked at least twenty hours at the bedside and were able to attend a two-day workshop. Thirteen participants were randomized to the resilience training arm and fourteen participants were randomized to a control group. The control group did not participate in any of the writing activities. Written informed consent was obtained from all participants and the study was approved by the Colorado Multiple Institutional Review Board.

Participants were asked to respond to writing prompts that were delivered weekly by the study team for twelve weeks. Writing prompts were delivered electronically; participant writing sessions lasted twenty to thirty minutes and were typed directly into an electronic database. The weekly writing prompts will be discussed in more detail later in this chapter.

Because of the sensitive nature of the writing prompts, an "honest broker" was used for this study. An honest broker is an individual who is not associated with the study team. The honest broker assigned unique study identification numbers to participants, which allowed them to access an electronic database to enter the weekly writing sessions anonymously. The study team could then access the writing samples without knowing the identity of the participant and offer feedback or guidance for future writing.

Within one week of completing the twelve-week intervention period, participants were asked to complete a satisfaction survey related to the writing component of the program. The Client-Patient Satisfaction Questionnaire-8 (CSQ-8) (Larsen et al. 1979) is an eight-item measure of satisfaction that is rated on a four-point Likert scale, with higher scores indicating greater satisfaction. There was also an open-ended question that allowed participants to include feedback to improve the writing sessions.

Transcript data was analyzed by two independent researchers, using qualitative theme analysis with subsequent development of central domains and subthemes via standard group processes. Afterward, the writing samples were reviewed again to assure congruency with the proposed themes.

Expressive Writing Intervention

The expressive writing intervention consisted of two parts. The first was a one-day workshop designed and facilitated by Evans and Jooste. The second was a twelve-week online expressive writing intervention consisting of a weekly writing prompt to which participants responded and received feedback from the workshop designers and facilitators.

One-Day Writing Workshop

This workshop, held at the University of Colorado Hospital in Denver/ Aurora, was divided into morning and afternoon two-hour sessions. In the morning session, the participants experienced an adapted implementation of the Pennebaker Paradigm (Pennebaker 2004). After a break for lunch, the participants attended a two-hour slide presentation exploring the characteristics of resilience and experienced the power of writing as a tool to build resilience.

Morning Session: The Pennebaker Paradigm
The Pennebaker Paradigm is a writing intervention developed by psychologist James Pennebaker consisting of four prompts. In Pennebaker's original study (1990), prompts were given to study participants on four consecutive days. The same prompt is used for the first two days; on the third and fourth days, the prompts differ slightly with an emphasis on changing perspective and making meaning while moving past, or successfully incorporating, the traumatic event into the life narrative. In the original study, participants were instructed to respond to each prompt for twenty minutes. The findings from the study indicate that this exercise promotes psychological resilience and

well-being by being both a cathartic expressive experience and an experience through which perspective is changed and meaning is elicited.

We adapted this intervention by using the four prompts in a two-hour session. As the first and second prompts are the same, our participants responded to them only once. They then responded to Prompt Three and Prompt Four separately, writing for twenty minutes each time. This exercise

Prompts for the Pennebaker Paradigm

Expressive Writing Prompt One and Two: In your writing, I would like you to really let go and explore your very deepest emotions and thoughts about the most traumatic experience in your entire life. You might tie this trauma to other parts of your life: your childhood, your relationships with others, including parents, lovers, friends, relatives, or other people important to you. You might link your writing to your future and who you would like to become, or to who you have been, who you would like to be, or who you are now.

Not everyone has had a single trauma, but all of us have had major conflicts or stressors and you can write about these as well. All your writing is confidential. There will be no sharing. Do not worry about form or style, spelling, punctuation, sentence structure, and grammar.

Expressive Writing Prompt Three: Now shift your writing so that you are considering the topic from a different perspective or different point of view. Write about how this event shaped your life and who you are. Explore, especially those deep issues about which you may be particularly vulnerable.

Expressive Writing Prompt Four: Now stand back and think about the events, issues, thoughts, and feelings that you have disclosed. Really be honest with yourself about this upheaval and do your best to wrap up your writing about this topic in a meaningful story that you can take with you into the future (Pennebaker 2004).

was followed by a presentation on the use of expressive writing as a tool to build psychological and emotional resilience and well-being. Pennebaker's work was described. The participants concluded this session by writing a reflection on their experience of the Pennebaker Paradigm exercise and shared their reflections in a group discussion.

In our workshop, participants did not share their writing. They did, however, as the final exercise of this session, complete a post-writing reflection. In this they wrote about the experience of responding to the prompts of the Pennebaker Paradigm, and the insights gained through this exercise. These reflections were then discussed as a group at the conclusion of the morning session.

Afternoon Session: Resilience—Surviving and Thriving in the Face of Change
With a slide presentation/demonstration, Evans and Jooste described the characteristics of resilience. Writing prompts were used as tools to build these resilience characteristics in the participants. To conclude the workshop, participants wrote a reflection on the writing experience and then shared these reflections in a group discussion. This practice—reflecting on the experience of writing—further augments the development of resilience within the writer. A further goal of the expressive writing experiences was to teach the method so that participants could use writing as a lifelong tool to promote their own resilience.

Our primary goal for the slide presentation/demonstration session was to introduce the participants to activities that improve the capacity for resilience. This included creating a vision for resilience; defining characteristics of resilience; demonstrating two forms of writing that overcome obstacles to resilience; teaching three forms of writing that build resilience; identifying personal qualities of resilience; and affirming growth in resilience.

We believe resilience entails learning how our mind-body connections serve us in our work; how to practice mindfulness and learning the power of language. Perspective is a great part of resilience training and healing.

Five types of writing were used in our presentation to develop resilience: expressive writing, transactional writing, poetic writing, affirmative writing, and legacy writing. In our workshops, we have found expressive and transactional writing useful in overcoming obstacles to resilience while poetic, affirmative, and legacy writing build resilience.

To prepare participants for resilience work, we asked them to write for one minute in answer to the question, "what does resilience mean for you?" Then we invited them to "reflect on what you just wrote. List several characteristics of resilience you are willing to share." Participants often described resilience in metaphoric language such as "standing as a tall oak tree," "steady as a grandfather clock," or "like a kaleidoscope, naturally and creatively adapting, different but still beautiful." These useful metaphors served as touchstones throughout the presentation and follow-up.

In the slide presentation, our central metaphor for resilience was the spider web. On a pound-for-pound basis, it's stronger than steel. It's a flaw tolerant system that can stretch and soften at first when pulled, and then stiffen again as the force of the pulling increases. It's the silk's unusual combination of strength and stretchiness and its ability to function mechanically well even when flawed, that make it the perfect metaphor for resilience (Chandler 2012).

Next we talked about examples of resilient people such as Nelson Mandela, Viktor Frankl (2006) and Megan and Barton Cutter (2013). We discussed the main characteristics of resilient people, who

- Are optimistic. They have faith in their own strength and their ability to overcome a problem.
- Are curious, focus on the present, experiment, wonder, and see new possibilities.
- Have faith in themselves to overcome difficulties. They often have a spiritual practice.
- Are connected to what is most important to them (their values) and see meaning and purpose in what they do.
- Have a vision for their life, based on values.
- Focus on that which they can control or change.
- Take responsibility for their physical well-being.
- Have a strong social network and a deep sense of connection.
- Are assertive and able to seek for and ask for what they need or desire.
- Have a sense of humor.
- Seek solutions when problems arise and can tolerate ambiguity and uncertainty until they find a solution.
- Are service-oriented.
- Experience and express gratitude.

Transformative Qualities for Writing for Health

Our workshop discussion focused on expressive writing as a way of building resilience. Referring to DeSalvo's *Writing as a Way of Healing: How Telling Our Stories Transforms Our Lives*, we instructed participants that DeSalvo, building on twenty years of research, suggests writing for health:

- Renders our experience concretely, authentically, explicitly, and with a richness of detail.
- Links feelings to events.
- Is a balanced narrative.
- Reveals the insights achieved from our painful experiences.
- Reflects upon the significance of what happened.
- Tells a complete, complex, coherent story. (1999, 57–61)

Participants were then directed to "Write about someone in your life—a friend, a colleague, a relative, or anyone else you can think of—who exhibits resilience."

One goal for the one-day writing workshop intervention was to expose participants to expressive, transactional, poetic, affirmative, and legacy writing prompts. Thus they were introduced to the types of writing used in the twelve-week follow-up. Another goal of the workshop was to describe resilience and provide characteristics and examples of resilience. Parallel goals were to enable participants to identify their own resilience, to perceive the power of their perspectives, thoughts, and language, and to enable them to experience the power of writing as a tool to build resilience.

The day ended with reminders about why we write:

- to create resilience in the face of change;
- to express our deepest feelings;
- to create metaphors that change our perspective;
- to tell stories that make sense of our lives;
- to communicate to others what needs saying;
- to take care of unfinished business;

- to affirm our core values; and
- to build resilience for ourselves and for those we love.

Twelve-Week Expressive Writing Follow-Up

For twelve weeks following the one-day writing workshop intervention, participants were sent a writing prompt and instructions for writing. Participants were asked to read the prompts and instructions and spend at least twenty minutes writing their responses. They then posted their writing in the secure designated environment. They were also encouraged to write and post a reflection about the assignment.

Week One

Here are your topic choices:

1. What is the most significant emotional experience you have faced and resolved in the last six weeks? Describe what happened, how you resolved it, and how you feel about it now.
2. What is something related to your most significant emotional experience that you are still thinking or worrying about too much? Describe what

Instructions for Weeks 1–4

Select one of the prompts offered and write about this experience for twenty minutes in the environment dedicated to this project. In your writing, really let go and explore your very deepest emotions and thoughts about your experience. Do not worry about form or style, spelling or punctuation, sentence structure or grammar.

you think about and how you feel about yourself when you have these thoughts.

3. What is something related to your most significant emotional experience that you have dreamed about at least once or often? Describe the dream. Describe how you feel in the dream and how do you feel when you recall the dream.

4. What is something related to your most significant emotional experience that you feel is affecting your life in an unhealthy way? Write about how it feels to tell this story about yourself.

5. What is something related to your most significant emotional experience that you have been trying to avoid thinking about for days, weeks, or years? What do you do to avoid thinking about it? On the occasion that you do think about it, describe how that feels.

Week Two

Here are your topic choices:

1. Write about a recent challenge you have had in your personal or professional life. In your writing, tell how you feel about the challenge and what it means to you.

2. Write about a recent time when you learned something vital to your personal or professional life. In your writing, tell how you feel about this learning and what it means to you.

3. Write about a recent time when you experienced a conflict of interest in your personal or professional life. In your writing, tell how you feel about this conflict of interest and what it means to you.

Week Three

Week Three's instructions repeated the Week Two prompts. Subjects were encouraged to choose a different prompt from the Week Two list.

Week Four

Here are your topic choices:

1. Write about a sensitive subject in your personal or professional life that you have been ruminating about for some time. In your writing, tell how

you feel about the sensitive subject and what it means to you. Write about how you may resolve this sensitive topic in a way that is comfortable for your moving beyond it.

2. Write about a recent time when you had a conflict of loyalty which consumed a lot of emotional energy. In your writing, tell how you feel about this conflict of loyalty and what it means to you. Write about how you may resolve this conflict of loyalty in a way that is comfortable for your moving beyond it.

3. Write about a recent time when you felt incapacitated in your personal or professional life. In your writing, tell how you feel about this time when you felt incapacitated and what it means to you. Write about how you may resolve this time of feeling incapacitated in a way that is comfortable for your moving beyond it.

Week Five

Instructions

Read the three options below and choose the *one* that serves your purposes best. Or you may decide to combine elements from each option, but you only need to write one twenty-minute letter for this assignment.

Choice # 1—The Compassionate Letter

Imagine if someone you love, your closest friend, your child, your partner, or your significant other had suffered the same trauma or traumas you wrote about in your expressive writing assignment.

In a compassionate and respectful way, write a letter with the advice you would have for them from your experience. You might also

- write about what you wish you had known but learned and what you imagine that they might be able to learn from the event;
- write about what ways you are now growing and that they may grow;
- write about any way that there was a benefit to the crisis;
- write about what your loved one might have learned about himself or herself from going through this difficulty;
- or you may write about all the above.

As you continue to respond to your loved one, write encouraging words of hope, comfort, and advice.

Choice #2—The Empathetic Letter

Symbolically take your leave of the past and move forward by composing a letter to yourself or to someone else involved in the distressing event that you described in your previous expressive writing assignments. Try to understand why this person did, said, or acted the way he or she did. You aren't saying what happened is right, just, or fair, but are instead trying to understand and empathize. Start from the assumption that the person isn't a bad person, but just did something that hurt you or that you don't understand. What could they have been thinking? What could have happened to them in the past to make them do what they did? What could they have felt as they did it, and what did they feel afterward? How do they feel now?

Choice #3—The Gratitude Letter

Write a letter to someone in your life whom you would like to thank for something they gave you, or something they taught you, or something they have inspired in you. Get right to the point and don't apologize for not writing before now. Describe your relationship with the person you are thanking and the context for this occasion. Describe the gift that you received, the skill you learned, or the inspiration you received from knowing him or her. In your letter tell what the gift meant to you when you received it. Tell how you felt about it then and now. Explain how you have been able to use this gift, or the skill, or the inspiration you received. Explain how your life has been enriched by what you have received and by his or her presence in your life.

Week Six

Poetic pre-writing exercise

[Participants are instructed to take several deep, relaxing breaths.]

Take a few minutes now to write about your day. Relax and just let the words come naturally. Do not worry about form. Just let the words come. Turn off the inner critic. Be mindful of your pen or pencil moving across the page or be mindful of words appearing across your computer screen as you press on the lettered keys. Let the room fall away and just focus on your writing.

Begin writing about your first thought as you lay in bed becoming awake. Describe your coming awareness of the new day before you got out of bed. What was your primary thought? How did you sleep? If you remember any dreams from last night, describe them. Describe any preoccupations that you may have had when you woke up in the morning. Describe your first glimpse of the day's weather as you got out of bed. How did you feel? Physically? Emotionally? Describe getting out of bed and how you felt. Describe your morning preparations as you got ready for your day. Describe what you had to eat for breakfast. Write about your morning activities. What did you do that you enjoyed? Describe your lunchtime. Did you eat alone? What did you eat? Drink? What was the best part? Write about your afternoon. Write about your drive to be here tonight. What did you think about on the drive or ride here? Describe any music or radio program you may have listened to or describe your interior monologue. What does it mean for you to be here? What plans do you have for when you get home? What plans do you have for the near future? How do you feel about these plans?

[Jane Kenyon's poem "Otherwise" (2003) is provided for participants.]

Consider the poem's lines, rhythm, and structure as providing scaffolding for your own poem. Substitute words appropriate for you and read your poem aloud to yourself. Consider anything you wish to change and revise as you wish.

Week Seven

[Langston Hughes's story "Salvation" (2013) is provided for participants.]

To complete this assignment, read this story and write a short reflection about what you think is going on in this story. Continue by writing a short creative nonfiction piece about a personal experience you had where you were unable or unwilling to complete a family rite of passage or fulfill family expectations. Bring your essay up to date by concluding with what you think about this now, and how you incorporate this story about yourself into the fabric of your identity and your life.

Week Eight

Affirmative Writing 1.0

In as much detail as possible, write about these three areas of your life.

Physical: What is your current state? What is your desired outcome?

Mental/Emotional: What is your current state? What is your desired outcome?

Spiritual: What is your current state? What is your desired outcome?

Affirmative Writing 1.1

Use the following questions to express things you wish to affirm for yourself.

- What do you look like at your personal best six months from now?
- What is the image that comes to your mind?
- Describe your face and your state of mind it reflects.
- How do you feel?
- How is your mood? What is your self-talk about these days?
- Describe your diet. Your habits. Your sleep. Your regular activities.
- How would you describe your interactions with others? Your relationships? Your work?
- How do you spend your time?

Now, write about your future self, only in the present tense. For example:

> *I am a vigorous, energetic person with a calm demeanor. My face, though older, has an ageless quality about it like some people of a certain age whose eyes usually have a slight glint of humor or quiet amusement. People tell me I look calm and peaceful. I feel a quiet strength and balance in my life. My diet is filled with good but simple natural ingredients including a glass of wine now and then. I exercise, meditate, and write regularly. I enjoy my family and friends. I am grateful that I am more mindful of life's wonders every day.*

Week Nine

Affirmative Writing 2.0: Writing that affirms your strengths

People's lives are transformed when they learn what their strengths/gifts are and when they nurture and practice those gifts. Every one of you has a certain gift or gifts. Some are evolving strengths/gifts like old friends that continue adapting to meet new challenges and situations. Some are resurfacing gifts, again like an old friend who has come back into your life just at the right time. Some are emerging gifts like a new friend who you wish to join in creating something special. Perhaps you have a number of gifts that may be asking for you to identify and express them.

Some people think about gifts as various religious traditions teach, and others are less specific, but think of a gift as a source of energy expressing itself through your spirit, essence, soul as: *you*! This power is expressing through you when you use your gifts because every gift has its own intelligence and wishes as it expresses through you.

Gifts are abilities that come to us naturally, that we just do as a natural expression of who we are. They may have come to us naturally, or we may have learned them as skills that only seem to come naturally now. It doesn't matter how we acquired or acquire our gifts, naturally or learned; the effect of a gift is the same. It is always win/win. A gift blesses the one who expresses the gift, and it blesses the one who receives its effects. The expression of a gift is free of outside expectations. We can choose which gift or gifts come to the foreground and later recede into the background. We can develop our gifts.

Here are some examples of strengths/gifts:

- Seeing possibilities in any situation
- Seeing beauty in everything
- Seeing others' potential
- Identifying core issues quickly
- Seeing patterns and connecting the dots
- Translating complex ideas and theories
- Inspiring others

Please write answers to the following questions:

- What are your strengths/gifts? List your gift or gifts like the examples above.
- What gift do you feel is ready to emerge, evolve, or resurface?
- How have you denied or hidden any gift in the past?
- How is your life and others' impacted when you withhold your gift?
- How might your life or others' be impacted if you offered your gift?
- What might living in this gift look like and feel like?
- What support from others do you need to develop your gift?
- What does your gift need from you?

After you have written answers to these questions about your gift or gifts, write a reflection about your gifts. Include in your reflection any gift that you feel is evolving, emerging, or resurfacing and your plans to offer this gift to the world.

Week Ten

Write about a joyous, happy, exuberant time in your life. It may be something recent or long ago. It may be about something you did or something someone did for you or with you. It may be a personally joyous occasion or one that happened at or through your work. The main idea is to write about a very happy, satisfying time. Describe how you felt then, and how you feel now remembering and writing about this time. Write about what you said or others said to you or about you at the time, and what you did to celebrate the happy occasion. Write about this satisfying time as if you are sharing the news with someone you care about deeply.

Week Eleven

Write for twenty minutes about one of these ideas or all of them, if you choose.

- How you wish to be remembered
- How someone has been a blessing for you
- How you have been a blessing for someone
- How you are making a positive difference in someone's life
- How you celebrate life

Week Twelve

Write for twenty minutes about one of these ideas, or both of them, if you choose.

1. Write about one thing you discovered about your life, your work, yourself in these twelve weeks of writing for resilience.
2. Write about one commitment that you intend to make going forward as a result of these twelve weeks of writing for resilience.

Results, Conclusions, and Suggestions for Further Study

Results

There was 100 percent completion of the writing assignments with a total of 156 writing sessions reviewed from the thirteen ICU nurse participants. Participants reported a high level of satisfaction with the writing portion of the program with CSQ-8 scores of 22.62 (SD± 8.08; range = 11–32). When providing written feedback about the program, participants reported that writing intervals were too frequent and they would have been more satisfied with biweekly sessions. Additionally, they reported a perception that there would be greater benefit in writing about traumatic work experiences and stress related to work instead of personal experiences.

Qualitative theme analysis of the writing samples identified four major domains associated with work-related trauma or work-related stress:

1. Systems/work structures, including subthemes related to problems with understaffing and working frequent night shifts.
2. Patient-centric, including subthemes related to feelings of injustice, death and dying, futile interventions, and stressful patients or family members.
3. Workplace relationships, including themes related to conflicts with colleagues as well as difficulties with interpersonal boundaries.
4. Cognitive processing, including themes of rumination and feelings of guilt or regret.

Conclusion

Expressive writing or written exposure therapy is a feasible and acceptable component to include in resilience training for critical care nurses. We were also able to identify domains and subthemes related to traumatic events experienced at work by ICU nurses. Since the writing sessions were only one component of this multimodal resilience intervention, it is difficult to assess the overall impact of writing in this context to improve resilience and mitigate symptoms of PTSD, BOS, anxiety, and depression. However, many of the participants in the study wrote reflections such as the one below about expressive writing that describes their perceptions of its usefulness.

> *One thing I discovered about myself is that I have the ability to be resilient as a nurse and as a human being. Before taking part in the study I felt like I was anxious all of the time, and that I worried continuously about my abilities as a nurse. Once I realized that all nurses share my same fears and anxieties it became much easier to address them. I found that the expressive writing helped me to recognize cognitive dissonance within myself, and also allowed me to see past areas of my life that are still a source of anxiety. By writing about both my fears and my joys I was able to move past my fears and be present in the moment occurring now. It also allowed me to see the joy in all situations, and to accept them without needing to change them.*

Suggestions for Further Study

Larger, randomized clinical trials are needed to determine the effect of the intervention on improving psychological outcomes. Research examining which writing prompts are more useful in overcoming barriers to resilience and which writing prompts build resilience is needed. More studies of expressive writing over time focused on work-related issues may provide guidance for adapting this model of intervention for other types of stressful occupation.

References

Chandler, D. 2012. How spider webs achieve their strength. *MIT News*, February 2.

Cutter, S. B., and M. Cutter. 2013. *Ink in the wheels: Stories to make love roll.* Raleigh, NC: Cutter's Edge Consulting.

DeSalvo, L. 1999. *Writing as a way of healing: How telling our stories transforms our lives.* San Francisco: Harper.

Frankl, V. 2006. *Man's search for meaning.* Boston: Beacon Press.

Hughes, L. "Salvation." English 103. Accessed January 3, 2013. http://www.courses. vcu.edu/ENG200-dwc/hughes.htm.

Larsen, D., C. Attkisson, W. Hargreaves, and T. Nguyen. 1979. Assessment of client/ patient satisfaction: Development of a general scale. *Evaluation and Program Planning* 2:197–207.

Kenyon, J. 2003. "Otherwise." Poemhunter. Accessed November 16, 2014. http:// www.poemhunter.com/poem/otherwise/.

Mealer, M., E. Burnham, C. Goode, B. Rothbaum, and M. Moss. 2009. The prevalence and impact of post-traumatic stress disorder and burnout syndrome in nurses. *Depress Anxiety* 26:1118–126.

Mealer, M., J. Jones, J. Newman, K. McFann, B. Rothbaum, and M. Moss. 2012. The presence of resilience is associated with a healthier psychological profile in intensive care unit (ICU) nurses: Results of a national survey. *International Journal of Nursing Studies* 49:292–99.

Pennebaker. J. 1990. *Opening up: The healing power of expressing emotions.* New York: Guilford.

———. 2004. *Writing to heal: A guided journal for recovering from trauma and emotional upheaval.* Oakland, CA: New Harbinger.

Smyth, Joshua M., J. Hockemeyer, and H. Tulloch. 2008. Expressive writing and post-traumatic stress disorder: Effects on trauma symptoms, mood states, and cortisol reactivity. *British Journal of Health Psychology* 13(1):85–93.

4

Writing the Darkness

A Transformative Writing Model

SHERRY REITER

For every survivor of severe trauma, there exists a *before* and an *after*. Events such as natural disasters, holocausts, war, accidents, rape, and other forms of violence leave indelible prints on the victims. The protective bubble of invulnerability that helps us to feel safe on a daily basis has been perforated. A survivor lives with the constant fear that all that is dear may disappear.

One definition of trauma states that "any wrenching or disturbing experience, especially one causing a disturbance in normal functioning" may be referred to as trauma (Webster 1990, 1419). The definition implies that it would be impossible to live without experiencing trauma; even a painful trip to the dentist, an argument with a loved one, or the loss of a job may be deemed traumatic by the one who suffers. Milder forms of trauma do not usually cause posttraumatic stress disorder (PTSD), memory impairment, or dissociation, three frequent responses to more severe trauma, but they share many symptoms of traumatic stress.

The Diagnostic Statistical Manual DSM-V (American Psychiatric Association 2013) is clear in its criteria. Diagnostic criteria for traumatic stress include events that meet specific stipulations and symptoms from each of four symptom clusters: *intrusion, avoidance, negative alterations in cognitions and mood,* and *alterations in arousal and reactivity.* Symptoms of intrusion, for example, may include numbing, hypervigilance, and involuntary memories through flashbacks or nightmares. Negative alterations in cognition and mood may include detachment and diminished interest in activities of living. Alterations in arousal and reactivity may include exaggerated startle responses or panic attacks. Persistence of trauma-related emotions (such as depression, anger, fear, shame, or guilt) color interactions with others.

The brain does not process a life-threatening event through the usual neural pathways. Instead, the most primitive part of the brain, the amygdala, is activated, and it floods the body with adrenaline and other hormones to maximize speed, strength, and chances of survival (MacCurdy 2000). The chief disadvantage of this hard-wiring is that the survivor has little or no recall of what happened.

Judith Herman (1992) said that traumatic memory is stored in "indelible image" (38); however, these images are without context. Herman was one of the first to describe the therapeutic process with trauma victims as beginning with reconstructing the story:

> Out of the therapeutic fragmented components of frozen imagery and sensation, patient and therapist slowly reassemble an organized, detailed verbal account.[1] A narrative that does not include the traumatic imagery and bodily sensations is barren and incomplete. (177)

Feldman et al. (1994) have suggested that there are four stages or phases of writing in trauma: *defensive, conventional, conflictual,* and *authentic.* The trauma survivor may start the process reluctantly (*defensively*), then become more *conventional* or referential and vague (e.g., "it was really awful.") *Conflictual* writing expresses the contradictions and paradoxes and eventually moves the trauma victim toward the final healing phase of acceptance and authenticity. In the *authentic* phase, the writing speaks through specific, concrete detail married to imagery; the logic of the left brain and the imagery and meaning-making of the right brain are working in whole-brain learning and processing.

This chapter reviews the ten elements of transformative writing (Reiter 2009)[2] and their relevance to trauma as a change agent. It includes specific case studies of writing for physical and psychological survival. Scientists traditionally suggest that the usual responses to stress are fight, flight, and freeze. Transformative writing represents an alternative coping response to stress. No fight, no flight—just write!

The Ten Principles
of Transformative Writing

The ten principles of transformative writing are not rules; rather they are observable components, particularly effective in the treatment of trauma because they address the specific symptomatology discussed earlier. The first four components—mastery, ritual, safety, and freedom—are the prerequisites that set the stage for the last six elements to occur.

Principle 1: Mastery

Writing is a form of empowerment. In many civilizations, there was a strong belief that to name someone or something was to magically possess it or have power over it. Remember the story of Helen Keller? (Keller et al. 2003) When her teacher first spells out W-A-T-E-R, a whole new world opens up. Helen is deliriously happy and runs from object to object as her teacher spells out their names. With her new mastery, she is able to organize her world and understand that each thing has its place. Similarly, writing can help identify and organize thoughts and feelings.

How does making little black squiggles on a sheet of paper help with wrestling the demons of trauma? Writing gives the survivor a locus of control. If a trauma victim can reduce the demon to the size of a page, it validates the fact that the individual is much bigger than the problem itself. By finding the words to reconstruct experience and create some meaning out of it, the survivor becomes victor rather than victim.

Principle 2: Ritual

Whenever human beings have been faced with change, whether alone or in groups, we create rituals to give significance to life transitions and reduce anxiety (Achterberg and Dossey 1994). Rituals acknowledge deep feelings, as well as the need for connection to self, community, and the sacred. Writing circles lend themselves beautifully to this ritual, and they are a natural re-creation of ancient healing circles where words were used for prayer and dialogue with the sacred. Traditionally, humans have always created rites of passage for birth, puberty, menopause, marriage, and death. Certainly extreme experiences deserve to be acknowledged through ritual or a ceremonial process. Writing can serve as a consistent ritual, marking the pain and triumph over moments where one's humanity and existence have been challenged.

Principle 3: Safety

James Dickey once called poetry the "last refuge of non-manipulative language" (Pies 1988, 85). The therapeutic notebook or journal becomes a safe sanctuary for all thought, whether in poetry or prose. When language is not focused on communicating with others, it may function as a way of communicating with the self. Because this communication is done in private, without any need to please or impress others, it is free of external judgment and absolutely safe from outside criticism. The words are for the writer's eyes alone. Only the writer decides if they are to be shared with a friend, a partner, or a therapist.

Even if the writer chooses not to share, the writing may serve as an extension of self (Leedy and Reiter 1981). The journal can serve as a trusted friend, alleviating a feeling of loneliness. The aim is to create an intimate relationship with oneself. Like any intimate relationship, confidentiality, honesty, and permission to be in a judgment-free space are required. Trust of self will grow when the person chooses a therapist or writing circle that feels "safe." Safety is a prerequisite for transformative writing and is paramount in counteracting the impact of violated or threatened boundaries that occurs with trauma.

Principle 4: Freedom

Family therapist Virginia Satir presented "five freedoms" (Staik 2011):

- the freedom to see and hear what is present instead of what should be, was, or will be;
- the freedom to feel what you feel instead of what you "should" feel;
- the freedom to say what you think and feel instead of what you ought to think and feel;
- the freedom to ask for what you want instead of always waiting for permission; and
- the freedom to take risks on your own behalf instead of choosing to be only "secure" and not rocking the boat. (2)

According to Satir, every person is entitled to these five freedoms. Trauma, by definition, is the involuntary exposure to a life-threatening situation, a violation of one's basic will to survive—a complete antithesis to freedom. One task of trauma recovery is to reclaim these essential freedoms and any others that may have been sacrificed.

Writing is restorative in its freedom to choose a "poetic" act. (*Poesis* means *creation*, to do or act.) The writer has the freedom to write a different story, or a different ending to the current story. The writer has the freedom to imagine a future that is made whole. The writer has the freedom to choose content, form, style, timing, and audience.

In addition, freedom is generous, forgiving, and accepting of contradictions. Freedom allows us to feel all of our feelings, anxiety to zest, and accept them all. As Walt Whitman wrote in his poem "Song of Myself":

Do I contradict myself?
Very well then, I contradict myself.
I am large. I contain multitudes. (Whitman 1926, 76)

Never underestimate the power of poetic license!

Principle 5: The Magic of the Poetic

Poetic devices include metaphor, rhythm, rhyme, alliteration, and a myriad of poetic tools and forms that are expressive and visceral. The therapeutic effect of poetic device is the creation of a form so pleasing to the mind that, whether through beauty or puzzle, the literature bypasses our natural resistance and can permeate the subconscious. One important poetic device is imagery or symbol. In art, the symbolic is portrayed in image; in poetry, the image is called metaphor. Metaphor is like the drawbridge permitting us to enter the castle of the psyche where the deeper realms of feeling and thought reside.

Transformation of time, space, and matter are also forms of poetic device that release us from ordinary, everyday restrictions. These transformations permit the trauma survivor to return to memories of the past or project himself into the future. The present reality is suspended to represent a truth that is significant and feeds the hunger for meaning that is innate in nearly every survivor.

Principle 6: Venting and Containment

Once words are externalized, they are simultaneously contained and expressed. Expression is vital in emotional regulation, as is containment. How the words are released, to whom they are released, and how the words are contained all contribute to safety, a sense of mastery, and poetic license. People recovering from trauma suffer from emotional dysregulation, including mood swings or poorly regulated emotional responses; therefore the use of poems and structured writing exercises facilitated by a trained biblio/poetry therapist can slowly and gently provide opportunities for releasing material when the individual chooses. The Journal Ladder (Adams 2013) will prove to be helpful in the structuring, containment, and pacing of the story.

When words, like emotions and memories, are invisible, they are infinitely more threatening than when they are safely held and anchored in a journal to be revisited any time the writer chooses. But first they must be externalized and made visible. The French writer Jean Cocteau (1930) kept a journal, *Opium: The Diary of His Cure*, to help him through the pain and anguish of recovery. The experience "would have dissolved leaving no other trace behind except a deep depression, if a fountain pen had not given it a direction, relief and shape. . . . Thought made flesh" (19).

Principle 7: Creativity

If the moment of trauma is fundamentally an act of destruction, then writing serves symbolically as an act of creation. It is an undoing of the near-annihilation experienced by the trauma victim. On a psychological and spiritual level, creativity enables us to transcend our limitations. It kindles the imagination, fuels our dreams, and plants seeds of hope that are vital for our renewal. When we write, our natural creativity finds new ways to view ourselves and the world.

The reparative process that deals with trauma through the imagination and interpretation has been called "formulation." Robert Jay Lifton (1991) refers to formulation as a kind of "psychic rebuilding." The construction of certain inner forms or configurations serves as "a bridge between self and world" (525–26).

From an analytic perspective, writing is a defense against death anxiety. As Nietzsche (1982)—and pop singer Kelly Clarkson (2011)—put it, "What does not kill me makes me stronger." A pen may indeed be mightier than a sword. Creation trumps destruction with a flourish of empowerment.

Principle 8: Witnessing

Recording thoughts and feelings is a testament to one's life experience. We never see ourselves completely, but when the trauma victim writes, externalization permits the viewing of her thoughts and feelings. With witnessing, the observing ego may have new observations, reflections, and perspectives. The journal may be the first witness, the friend that reduces the sense of being alone in the pain. The journal never talks back and never judges. The writing may be shared with the therapist and groups for multiple witnesses to validate the event that has slipped past the conscious cognitive and emotional systems because it has been too large and dangerous to take in alone.

Writing about the trauma memorializes the moments of terrible vulnerability and the triumph over death and helplessness. Witnessing, a counterforce to annihilation, becomes possible when the traumatic experience is externalized, concretized, and preserved through transformative writing.

Principle 9: Integrating Parts into a Whole

Self-dialogue is part of the writing process. Through transformative writing, one permits oneself access to inner dialogue. The term "polyphonic dialogue" (Chance 2011) has been used to capture the idea of "many voices."

One part of the self asks questions; another part of the self answers, and yet another part of the self reflects and problem-solves. Writing can connect feelings and thoughts so the individual learns what it is that he knows. Self-expression, self-discovery, and self-understanding become possible through the externalization of writing and the observing ego.

A trauma victim may experience alienation, depersonalization, and dissociation. All ten aspects of transformative writing work together to review, renew, and reorganize the revolving door of fragmented images of severe trauma with meaning-making. Integrating the fragmented parts into a whole is the task of every trauma survivor.

Principle 10: Theory of Self and Relativity (Self-in-the-World)

The term "theory of self" is used to suggest a cohesive self-image in which the many aspects, voices, and images connect to each other and form an integrated whole, as discussed in Principle 9. Once the self is cohesive, connection to the larger world is possible. First one must connect with self; then connection with others can take place; these connections can help to shift the relationship that the victim has to his or her trauma.

Relativity or connection is the ability to relate and connect with the larger world. It is an important concept of wellness that tribal groups have always embraced, usually through symbol, ritual, and ceremony.

The articulation of self or self-expression will counter numbness and alienation, as will relating to significant others and the community at large. Those who struggle with their relations to other humans may choose to connect to a pet, the beauty of nature, or the Divine to counter feelings of disconnection.

The trauma victim's world sometimes constricts the inner world to two sole entities: the victim and the trauma. However, this tightly knit relationship can be penetrated by expressions of caring, empathy, and the support of family and friends.

Transformative Writing at Work: Case Examples

The Woman Who Built a Labyrinth with Words

Although we may believe our lives are mostly under our control, there are times when culture, legal systems, and community politics have the power to fragment personal narratives. If a family member is in crisis, her disrupted storyline completely alters every other family member's storyline. Such is the trauma of Susan, who seemed to be leading the ideal life, married to a handsome doctor, living in a beautiful home in the suburbs where they were raising their two lovely daughters. However, when Susan's husband, a pediatric neurologist, was accused of molesting his young patients, and imprisoned, their lives turned into a nightmare overnight.

> It is now six journals and three years since the night my husband was questioned in the parking lot outside his office. The image of Philip sobbing in my arms on the day he is released on bail is etched in my mind. His account comes

in broken words: orange jumpsuit, shackles, eating spaghetti with a plastic spoon. Almost overnight, he lost everything. The news and sensational media coverage escalated quickly. In a very short time, Philip's life resembled that of Job in the Bible. He encountered loss after loss: his name, his career, his integrity, his home, and watching his children growing up. Losses like this are only tolerable with a journal in hand. There is so little control or power I have right now to change the situation. However, in the writings, the flow of life experiences is fluid, moving between the past, the present, and the future, which is where our hope lies. (Reiter 2009, 183)

Time-shifting enabled Susan to feel unstuck despite a situation where "time is being served" and life may feel as though it is "on hold" (Principle 5).

The lack of mastery (Principle 1) and safety (Principle 3) scream out in her poem:

With their huffing-and-puffing
blow-your-house down
and the smoldering of our hearts
leaving us speechless,
I wait for the words
"It's safe now.
Okay to come out." (Reiter 2009, 191)

Susan wrote throughout her trauma. Putting pen to paper was a way of imposing a semblance of order and control over a situation that was beyond her comprehension (Principle 1).

Her words formed a labyrinth, an intricate maze of private passages in an effort to forge a path where none was evident. Susan wrote to bear witness to the truth as she knew it (Principle 8). Her truth was in direct conflict with that of the judicial system. In the journal she had full poetic license, the freedom to express what she could not voice anyplace else (Principle 4). The journal was a sanctum—free of wagging tongues, prying eyes, and judgment. Since her teen years, Susan established the ritual of turning to her journal for self-nurturance and identity affirmation (Principle 2).

She writes, "I had the safety of a lined page in a blank book [Principle 3]. I had time [Principle 4] to re-read myself and I found the understanding that I wanted from others" (Reiter 2009, 198).

Rereading is a function of time-shifting (Principle 5). Slowing down to digest her own words helps Susan to integrate thought, feeling, and experience (Principle 9). Finding the understanding that Susan wanted from others was part of her healing (Principle 9).

This expansion of time is especially important when the individual is trying to process a traumatic situation and integrate aspects of reality that are not ego-syntonic. Susan's integrity is challenged, but she is able to maintain a cohesive theory of self despite being threatened by others' perceptions and actions (Principle 10).

The magic of poetic device (Principle 5) is essential because Susan's experience cannot be contained in ordinary language. Note the many metaphors in the following passage, written in her journal:

> I have been slung from a slingshot of tragedy into the hemisphere of nothingness—that is what hurts. As if the cord between my husband and my daughters has been severed and each one of us is hurtling out into space in different directions. Some days my heart feels as if it will burn itself out like the end of a wick in a pool of melted wax. Some days Phillip's name is a bone caught in my throat. (Reiter 2009, 196)

Can the strokes of the pen rewrite the story? Writing ensures that Susan's story will not be consumed in her husband's drama. In the act of becoming the storyteller (Principle 1), she has the last word in a story that no one else can edit. Somehow, Susan will forge a path out of the labyrinth of words to eventually arrive in a new place, because she has never let go of her true voice—or her pen.

The Poem That Was a Prayer

Sister Mary first contacted me during a health crisis. In six weeks' time, she faced a delicate operation on a tumor winding around her nasal cavity that risked leaving her permanently disabled.

Sister Mary was already an experienced writer, and in our work together she was easily able to transition into bringing transformative principles to her expressive writing. First and foremost, she wrote for a sense of control (Principle 1) and self-regulation of emotion through catharsis (Principle 6). Writing served as a container to hold a kaleidoscope of feelings. Distance was needed from the onslaught of terror. Through writing her own poetry she was able to draw boundaries around her fear, to separate the disease from herself (Principle 1), and to contain the excessive emotion (Principle 6).

Tumor, you are you
Tumor, I am I
Tumor, I cannot let you define me. (Reiter 2009, 121)

By speaking directly to the tumor as though it were a being, Sister Mary used personification and poetic device (Principle 5) to witness her situation and obtain perspective (Principle 8). Externalizing this crisis in words made it available for reflection, witnessing (Principle 7), and problem solving. Because fear and anger tend to create disorder and chaos, Sister Mary was also writing for clarity, organization, and mastery (Principle 1). Through her confusion, anger, and grief, she continued to connect to the Divine (Principle 10) in her journal.

Sister Mary was having trouble sleeping. I suggested prescription poetry, the repetition of a peaceful poem said aloud before going to sleep. Sister Mary's choice was Jane Kenyon's poem "Let Evening Come" (1996), and it succeeded in helping her to relax.

The prescriptive poem served as a unit of energy, spiritual, emotional, and cognitive energy, imported and embraced by her open mind, open heart, and open spirit (Principle 9). Eli Greifer (1963, 2) would have called it a "psychograft—a transfusion of the soul." The poetry therapist may "import" a poem (offer a published poem, such as the Kenyon poem) or "export" a poem (bring out a poem from inside the client). Sister Mary benefited from both methods.

Sister Mary had her own personal code of significant symbols that were repeated throughout her poetry (Principle 5). The metaphor of water, "riptide dangerous," served to further encapsulate her terror and anger (Principle 6). In one of the first poems, "Nightmare," Sister Mary looks over a terrifying expanse of water. In a later poem, Sister Mary referred to her terror as a "sea of darkness," as she wrestled with her faith:

Faith lies under tiers
(under tears)
of doubt, distrust, discouragement

I cannot see
I need to take the hand
of a God Who sees
I need to wade with unhesitating trust
into this sea of darkness. (Reiter 2009, 126)

The health crisis is not only a crisis of the body; it is also a crisis of the soul. This crisis was a challenge to Sister Mary's theory of self, as well as a challenge to her church community, in which fear connotes lack of faith. Yet Mary maintained a strong connection with the Divine, as well as with her therapist (Principle 10).

Prior to the operation, Sister Mary wrote what she called her breakthrough poem, "Soundings," in which water continues to be central. However, the symbolism has changed; Sister Mary has become the boat, and the sea of darkness has transformed into a sea of God's love.

God sounds out my soul
tosses down a line
measures the depth of my faith
How far down before bottom reached
Are there fathoms enough to carry me to shore
Will I capsize
I snivel fear
cast a line up
into the heart of God
Trust with invincible hope
I will run out of line. (Reiter 2009, 127)

As Sister Mary explained to me, "running out of line" is a nautical term meaning the depth of water is so great that the ship can move freely. Here is what Sister Mary says about her "breakthrough poem":

All six weeks of laborious writing brought me to this moment. This was it. It was the peak, the crown of all my tears, struggles, fears, and words. A tremendous sense of power was awakened in me by my own words. It was my mantra. It was my prayer. I survived the operation. The tumor was benign. I recuperated with no impairments from the surgery. (Reiter 2009, 127)

The need for safety (Principle 3), mastery (Principle 1), containment, and release (Principle 6) are all accomplished through the ritual of writing and the magic of the poetic (Principle 5). Mary needed to feel free from the restrictions of the church and chose someone who was outside her faith instead of her spiritual director. Through her writing, she self-regulated her emotion, and with amazing mastery, conquered her fear. Perhaps most importantly, she continued to explore and strengthen her relationship with God in a poem that was, in fact, a prayer.

The Poem That Was Snake Medicine

Rarely does a poem take twenty-five years to complete. However, it took Preston, a Vietnam veteran, that long to create his poem "Rung Sat" because his mind withheld certain information, holding terrifying images hostage for more than two decades. During Preston's flashbacks, time and space shifted (Principle 5), as his memory unexpectedly took him back to Vietnam. In a series of starts and stops, the brain downloaded each image, often when least expected. In an act of mastery and creation (Principles 1 and 7), Preston was able to piece together his history (Principle 9).

The indelible images of his trauma insistently informed him of his experience, but without narrative. Therefore, until he could shape them into a poem, his senses of mastery, safety, and freedom were jeopardized. He was at the mercy of these images until he completed "Rung Sat." Preston writes:

> Curiously, more than a decade passed before memories started to surface. I had flashbacks and would awake shaking and in a sweat and screaming. At home, my anger unleashed itself as I yelled at my wife and children. As the years went on, more memories came back and I anchored them to the page by writing them out.
>
> It was a way of trying to understand what had happened. The war had become a blur. I had very little recall of actual events. Memories came back to me, piece by piece, like a jig-saw puzzle. I wrote only one poem when I was in Vietnam. In "Rung Sat" I tried to grasp the reality of this war. It was a collage of some of the experiences I had in Vietnam, and helped me to put things into perspective. It took me twenty-five years to rewrite this poem until I was finally satisfied. The poem is significant because it was the first time I was honest with myself about what I had done. The poem serves as a witness. (Reiter 2009, 46)

What follows is an excerpt from Preston's poem, "Rung Sat." Rung Sat is a jungle where the North Vietnamese Army (NVA) and Viet Cong (VC) entered South Vietnam. The words "orange mist" refer to Agent Orange, a chemical defoliant sprayed in Vietnam. The substance is now widely believed to be carcinogenic, but its toxicity was not known by many at the time. Preston suffered, as did many others, from sores, numbness, and circulation problems. Although the soldiers' faces were camouflaged, their hands and arms were exposed. They would live with the aftereffects of Agent Orange all their lives.

We demand revenge:
the smell of rice at the jungle top,
lazy orange mist shifting like smoke.
In low silhouette, we patrol to ambush
our bodies surrounded by dark
the shadow of surprise suspended inside us.
Across the trail, wind rips nipper palm,
fear crawling at our feet, like a wounded man.
We radio in an air strike
the wounded lie with the dying,
the dragged bodies, hurried away
disappear into bamboo.
Blood trails along the river
mark a company retreat—
abandoned bombed-out bunkers
shallow graves dug quickly,
brown-uniformed and black pajama bodies,
rice bowls and fish heads
children half-buried in dirt.
I am a man half in the water, half out;
my legs suck into mud.
My arms hold my head outstretched
hasten to deliver me among the dead. (Reiter 2009, 47–48)

When questioned about the line, "I am a man half in the water, half out," Preston said that this line captures the way he felt many years later—one foot in this world and one foot in the other:

I felt numb and half-dead when I was in Vietnam. Part of me was almost begging them to kill me. Like John the Baptist, I wanted to be delivered. I was tormented by guilt, but not yet conscious of that. This poem and the others I wrote serve as witness and testament. (Reiter 2009, 48)

When Preston externalizes the images by converting them to ink (Principle 1), he can view the toxic images at a safe distance (Principle 3). He is also able to stand back to witness the experience with new understanding (Principle 8). When he captures the image to his satisfaction, he is empowered. When he edits and re-edits, he exercises artistic freedom and control of the process (Principles 1 and 4).

While trauma separates the person from the world, writing can also be a statement to return the victim to the world. Writing workshops such as the William Joiner Center for War and Social Consequences Writer's Workshop have been very successful for veterans. By sharing among other veterans, Preston's trauma was not borne alone (Principle 10).

War is alienating, destructive, and fragmenting; writing is unifying, integrative, and opposes silence. Writing is an under-utilized tool that may assist veterans in moving through the necessary process of articulating the trauma, witnessing, mourning, and integration (Principles 1, 8, and 9).

The rattle of the snake is present in many of Preston's poems about the war. It is said that if one survives ingested snake poison, it is possible to transmute the toxins. Preston is absorbing and metabolizing the poison of his wartime experience, rendering it less toxic with each poem he writes. He is performing one of the most difficult of all transformations: the conversion of blood to ink.

Conclusion

Writing is like taking an emotional x-ray. It will reflect the thoughts and emotions of the traumatized person. At first these thoughts are fragmented and disorganized. With treatment, a reorganization will take place. Nonverbal creative arts therapies (art, dance, music, drama) may be used prior to the act of writing, until a readiness appears to work with narrative and words.

A trained facilitator will use highly structured, nonthreatening exercises to slowly move past resistance and referential writing (the story about the story) to authentic, vivid narrative.

The ten principles of transformative writing inform and sensitize practitioners to observable elements in the quest for restoration and creative healing. If we view posttraumatic stress disorder a condition of memory that is difficult to articulate, then it is the mental health professional's job to help the victim to articulate and reconstruct the narrative and its meaning in the victim's life. Transformative writing is a potent and valuable tool in the treatment of posttraumatic stress disorder.

References

Achterberg, Jeanne, and Barbara Dossey. 1994. *Rituals of magic: Using imagery for health and wellness.* New York: Bantam.

Adams, Kathleen. 2013. The journal ladder. In *Expressive writing: Foundations of practice*, edited by Kathleen Adams. Lanham, MD: Rowman & Littlefield, 43–50.

American Psychiatric Association. 2013. *Diagnostic and statistical manual of mental disorders, 5th edition: DSM- V.* Arlington, VA: American Psychiatric Publishing.

Baldwin, Christina. 1977. *One-to-one: Self-understanding through journal writing.* New York: Evans & Co.

Chance, Abigail. 2011. Polyphonic feminisms: Acting in concert. *The Scholar and the Feminist Online* 8(3). Accessed September 30, 2013. http://elevatedifference. com/review/polyphonic-feminisms-actin-concert-scholar-and-feminist-online-issue-83-summer-2010.

Clarkson, Kelly. 2011. *Stronger.* RCA Records, a division of Sony Music Entertainment. Accessed June 1, 2014. www.rcarecords.com/artists.

Cocteau, Jean. 1930. *Opium: The diary of his cure.* London: Peter Owen.

Feldman, Susan C., David Read Johnson, and Marilyn Ollayos. 1994. The use of writing in post-traumatic stress disorders. In *Handbook of post-traumatic therapy*, edited by Mary Beth Williams and John F. Sommers. Westport, CT: Greenwood, 366–85.

Greifer, Eli. 1963. *Principles of poetry therapy.* New York: Poetry Therapy Center.

Herman, Judith. 1992. *Trauma and recovery.* New York: Basic Books.

Keller, Helen, Roger Shattuck, Dorothy Herman, and Anne Sullivan. 2003. *The story of my life.* New York: Norton.

Kenyon, Jane. 1996. *Otherwise: New and selected poems.* Minneapolis, MN: Graywolf Press.

Leedy, Jack, and Sherry Reiter. 1981. The uses of poetry in drama therapy. In *Drama in therapy*, vol. 2, edited by Gertrud Schattner and Richard Courtney, 221–40. New York: Drama Book Specialists.

Lifton, Robert Jay. 1991. *Death in life: Survivors of Hiroshima.* Chapel Hill: University of North Carolina Press.

MacCurdy, Marion M. 2000. From writing to trauma: A theoretical model for practical use. In *Writing and healing: Toward an informed practice*, edited by Charles Anderson and Marion MacCurdy. Urbana, IL: National Council of Teachers of English, 158–200.

Nietszche, Frederich. 1982. Maxims and arrows, #8. In *The portable Nietszche*, edited by Walter Kaufmann. New York: Penguin. (Originally in *Twilight of the idols*, 1888.)

Pennebaker, James W., and Sandra K. Beall. 1986. Confronting a traumatic event: Toward an understanding of inhibition and disease. *Journal of Abnormal Psychology* 95(3):274–381.

Pies, Ronald. 1988. The poet and the therapist. In *Journal of Poetry Therapy* 2(2): 84–88.

Reiter, Sherry. 2009. *Writing away the demons: Stories of creative coping through transformative writing.* St. Cloud, MN: North Star Press.

Staik, Athena. 2011. The five freedoms of becoming fully human: Virginia Satir and mental health. *Neuroscience and relationships.* Accessed October 3, 2013. blogs. psychcentral.com/relationships/2011/05/the-five-freedoms-of-becoming-more-fully-human—virginia satir-mental-health/.

Webster, Daniel. *Random House Webster's college dictionary.* 1990. New York: Random House.

Whitman, Walt. 1926. *Leaves of grass.* Garden City, NY: Doubleday.

Notes

1. Herman's focus on a "detailed verbal account" is paralleled in the research correlating writing and wellness. The recall of specific details and images, and writing them down has been shown to be a factor in improving overall health and strengthening the immune system, starting with the earliest study (Pennebaker and Beall 1986).

2. The original set of principles in *Writing Away the Demons: Stories of Creative Coping through Transformative Writing* (Reiter 2009) has evolved over time and use. In the original set, Transformation of Time, Space, and Matter was a separate principle; it is now considered a subcategory of The Magic of the Poetic. The principle of Theory of Self and Relativity has been added as an important component in transformative writing. It is especially significant in the healing of traumatic stress, in which feelings of safety in relationship may be compromised.

5

Emotional Balance, the Journal, and the Therapy Session[1]

BETH JACOBS

Suppose you just received disturbing news and you feel very upset. Then suppose you are given a choice of going in a room where you can talk to a trained therapist for thirty minutes or going in a different room for the same thirty minutes where there is nothing but a desk with writing supplies. Which would you choose? Why?

Those two hypothetical half-hours are incomparable experiences, and fortunately, we rarely have to line them up as an either/or decision. But talk therapy and expressive/therapeutic writing are two of the most helpful tools people have to soothe emotion and center themselves. The differences between the two illuminate some of the benefits of each.

Although I have used journals for emotional balance throughout my life, I never considered the systematic implications of that practice until people I worked with in psychotherapy started talking about their own journals. I was surprised how many clients in my therapy practice kept journals. The two modes are certainly compatible; people in therapy tend to be verbal, internally inquisitive, and seeking change, as are journal writers. Graf's research (2004) found that 52 percent of people starting psychotherapy at an outpatient clinic had had some experience with journaling. My experience as a therapist is consistent with that. I have found there is an overlap between the groups of people who seek personal development through therapy and through writing.

As I worked with my clients, I listened carefully to their descriptions of their journals and why they were writing. The common theme that emerged was that emotional expression was spilling over from life onto the page. Journals were containing emotion that had nowhere to go. Sometimes this was because there were not people who could process affect with the writer, recalling Anne Frank's words in her diary, "Paper is more patient than man" (2001, 200). Sometimes clients just wrote because it was convenient, creative, or helpful in building boundaries by expressing without sharing. I started experimenting with giving people writing ideas to address specific emotional needs or to develop specific emotional skills. Within the psychotherapy context, I realized there was enormous and diverse therapeutic potential for journaling (Jacobs 2005).

I also started to have some interesting experiences in sessions that involved talking about people's journals. Each one taught me something more about the amazing world of personal writing. I named one such event "the ghost of journals past."

The Ghosts of Journals Past

The client was a beautiful young woman who kept her own feelings at arm's length all the time. Like many people who come to therapy, she found herself in the same situation over and over with different people, but she had no sense of her participation in the patterns of her life. The more she pushed aside how she felt, the less she could understand how once again her innocent flirtations led her to an affair with a married man at work. She had come to therapy to break out of this cycle that she barely recognized.

We talked a lot about her relationships, her family history, and how competitive feelings got stirred up at her job. We developed many good theories about her situation, all of which she accepted, but none of which led to any depth of feeling or change. She felt she just needed to change jobs again and see if that would help.

I was wondering what would get us to deeper feeling, to more of the vulnerability behind the predatory behavior, when a surprising thing happened. The client came in and handed me some pieces of paper. She told me she found some diaries from when she was sixteen years old and these were copies of some of their pages. There were sections highlighted in yellow. Her teenage words directly echoed our discussions but added the element of emotion that had got so buried over the years. "I don't know why I like to tease the boys so much. I know I do it all the time. I guess I just like that power. I never feel so important. It's the only time I know anyone notices me and thinks I'm cool."

There was her current reality in bubbly teenage script. How could it be that a questioning, sad, sixteen-year-old girl could plant a message to unlock her future self?

This story never stops fascinating me with its illustration of the multiplicity of the self. How is it that we can we surprise ourselves as we write and by our writing? By what process do we purposefully create an opening for what is not premeditated? This journal opened up an internal, emotional world where finally the work of change could commence.

Creating Client Rituals with Journaling

Another client loved to write in her journal and was near the end of therapy, but she was having trouble leaving the dependence of the therapeutic relationship and the sense of protection she felt in our weekly sessions. We devised an interesting exit plan using her journal. Every week she would write a selection for me or pick something out of her journal and hand it to me, and I would write brief responses to the material. I would often say little more than how much I liked how she put something or how it reminded me of a theme that we had worked on together over the course of her treatment. I discovered that I enjoyed reading her impressions of how our time together affected her.

Our exchange ritual at the beginning of the session grew to have great meaning. She handed me some paper with shredded spiral-ripped edges, and I handed back a piece of stationery with the prior week's commentary. We took a minute to peruse the messages and then start talking about what was happening in the present.

After a few months, it became clear that the client was ready to leave therapy and that her anxiety about discharge had decreased. We both attributed the change to the paper trail. Something about the concrete trade of material symbolized the exchange within our relationship: She could leave her worries, impressions, and point of view with me and I would hold them, and I could leave her with tokens of my appreciation of her as a person in a way that was finally internalized.

Releasing Emotional Blockages

Another story that evolved in psychotherapy was every journal writer's nightmare: the journal that is intruded upon. And this was in the worst possible circumstances. A woman was struggling with a sexual addiction that was completely unknown to her husband. She really loved her husband and desperately wanted therapy to help her, but she wrote about her conflicts and exploits and left her journal somewhere that her husband noticed. The ensuing revelation was devastating. The two of them came to my office for an emergency session, and the client finally confronted the emotional split in her. A long process of healing began at the point of the journal's confession.

My client and her husband began couples therapy and my client started realizing the true impact of her behavior. Because her secret world was brought to the light of day, she could no longer escape to it as a soothing fantasy. She started to build a more authentic relationship with her husband.

We sometimes wondered about the possibilities of unconscious intent in her leaving her journal where he might see it. We can never answer that question entirely, but it turned out that the journal was a vehicle to an integrated reality in many ways.

There were other less dramatic tales and uses of journals within the psychotherapy session. One client was a science writer who had trouble opening up to her emotions; we used journaling to help her develop a vocabulary for the range of feelings she had. Another client used her journal similarly, to help release emotional blockages. She would make me laugh at certain times, looking up at me and saying, "I guess it's time for the green notebook, right?" One client with obsessive-compulsive disorder used a journal to help her curb obsessive behavior, such as searching the Internet for information about her minor physical ailments until she became terrified of drastic diagnoses. She got a notebook and was instructed to write about her feelings for five minutes before turning on the computer; it helped her both minimize the behavior and understand its context.

Seeking Emotional Balance

Many of my clients shared variations of a single dominant dimension, over- and under-expression of emotion. There were definitely more clients who came in with piles of notebooks filled with emotional venting, and they tended to need some structuring to move the process along. Emotional venting can spiral out of control without some closure. I never discourage venting and believe it is almost always a necessary first step toward emotional balance, but I found that a page limit or a structured ending with some analysis or review helped these people. For example, the client might be invited to write:

- three questions that the writing leads him to ask; or
- a ten-word summary of the feeling expressed; or
- a reassurance she wishes someone could give her after hearing how she feels.

The under-expressers tended not to have words available for their inner sense, so they worked well with exercises that developed an emotional vocabulary. For instance, a client who was only able to provide a binary, black/white emotional scale ("I'm angry" or " "I'm not angry") might be offered an anger thermometer. The client would first describe a situation that made him as angry as he had ever been in his life, and ranked that as a 10 on a 0–10 scale. The scale would continue to be refined to develop a sense of the subtleties of feeling variations. The anger thermometer helps people recognize earlier stages of feelings as they develop, which is very useful for early intervention. Some clients benefit from writing about how they feel in nonfeeling terms, such as bodily sensations, types of music, or color.

"Control Is a Tough Nut"

All of my experiences with writing and as a therapist impressed me with the individuality of how people use journals and what journals help people develop at different times. Different writing ideas enhanced and developed different skills, and these skills could be generalized. What could be worked out on the page did have a bearing in life. But seeing the benefits of journaling within the therapeutic relationship also caused me to look at the themes and overlaps between these modalities.

An important point of connection is the common motivation to find more comfort with emotional life. The physical nature and urgency of emotion get beyond all of us at times, and similar struggles drive people to either therapy or the journal. What I heard most frequently in both contexts was a sense that feelings were interfering with life's course and satisfaction.

So, why exactly are emotions so difficult to manage? In the movie *Ordinary People*, the psychotherapist tells his young client, "Control is a tough nut." People in psychotherapy and in life often carry the misconception that we should be able to control our emotions.

Emotions are processes that occur spontaneously and organically. Even well-intentioned efforts to control emotions usually backfire and cause more damage than the feeling did in the first place. It works much better to try to understand the natural system of our emotions and to try to create circumstances where emotions are positive and manageable, and where decisions about feelings are well informed.

Understanding Emotional Balance

To understand emotional balance, it's important to start with understanding how emotions are processed in the brain. In human evolution, emotions seem to have developed to function like highlighters to text. They make certain stimuli jump out and stick with us. This probably had great survival value in a physically dangerous world where, for instance, learning what a predator looks like made a person afraid to go near the place where they last saw the creature. However, being afraid to talk to somebody because of painful inter-actions with similar characteristics in your past is not adaptive. The mecha-nisms of emotion wear thin in some current applications.

The flush of recognition and bodily reaction, combined with deeply per-sonal associations and interpretations, is what we call emotion. We remain hard-wired to take in certain stimuli, react and memorize them in a dominant way. There are several brain mechanisms that ensure we notice and react to emotional stimuli. First of all, the emotional circuits in the brain, the limbic system, are located in a deep and central loop in the cortex. They connect di-rectly to parts of the brain that receive and code information and associations. They can take in information about a stimulus from many sources, combin-ing different sensory and thought areas.

The emotional system also has vast output connections that activate sys-tems throughout the brain and body. The limbic system is close to memory storage, so once it is activated, learning is instantaneous. Limbic connections tie to the centers that regulate arousal, leading to the fight-or-flight phenom-ena of activation of heart rate, breathing, and sweating. They even connect directly to some hormonal glands, sending signals to the entire body that can last for days. Also, the limbic system releases neuromodulators, which are chemicals that affect neurons firing throughout the brain (LeDoux 2002).

Finally, the limbic system gives feedback to the attention-directing system of the brain to stay focused on the emotional stimulus (LeDoux 2002). That's part of why we get so riveted on emotional information and actually can't process other information that might be coming in to contradict the strong feeling that has been aroused. We might recall that the person who has hurt us sometimes acts quite kindly toward us, but at the moment of hurt we aren't thinking about that.

When an emotion is aroused, we are intensely involved with that process, and the neuron that is carrying information chemically through the emo-tional circuits is now trained to fire more easily the next time we encounter something related to this experience. The brain pathway to reacting wears down like ruts in a dirt road. It might seem overwhelming, and it certainly explains why at times emotions feel overwhelming. It's not just something we imagine. If we then decide our feelings are bad, we just tie in another path-way of self-criticism to our emotion and amplify its negative impact. Then, we often start trying to throw off the emotion, and processes of defense like projection and disavowal occur, which confuse people and lead to interpersonal disasters.

Given this complicated machinery of emotion, we all struggle throughout our development to learn skills of emotion management. Regulation is derived from our bodily states and builds up gradually through the medium of human interaction. All of our emotional processing is filtered throughout life by what we learn from every instant of interaction we experience. The permutations of how human interaction translates into a person's emotional system in the world vary infinitely. Each moment adds a complex layer of experience or information to our data collection.

As we develop, each skill we acquire causes us to rework and recalibrate our emotional worlds. As infants, our emotional regulation is largely tied to physical regulation, which is tied to caregivers' behaviors. From the beginning, emotional tones register with these behaviors. When toddlers first walk and move independently, they are capable of seeing for the first time that emotions exist as separate processes within their own and others' bodies. Suddenly they can move away from people and experience their own states as staying within their own bodies. This is a huge realization, still unarticulated verbally. The acquisition of verbal skills adds the paradigm shift of discrimination to these internal states; they have names and can be described and examined through language.

The next major step occurs with the development of abstract thought and exposure to other systems of emotion for school-age children. Once a child can mentally experiment with and manipulate emotional concepts, the possibilities of experience are endless. Children start to fantasize and experience created emotion and to recall and relive past emotion. Once children have relationships outside of their original environment, they also see how relative the world of emotions can be.

All of this time, the subtle and overt messages received in relationships deeply imprint our sense of what emotion is, how it can or cannot be expressed, and how we perceive our own experience of emotion and mind. Given the essential workings of our brain, most of the problems arise in the conflicts of our experience and interactions. Life's unavoidable troubles, mismatches within families, the persistence of history's confusions and losses always cause some obstruction of emotional experience.

It seems that the best overall expression of emotional balance is to allow emotion to run its course. The more we understand the physical reality of this process and the details of our own historical associations in the process, the more room we give it and we create less resistance and friction. It is hugely relieving if just a tiny corner of the brain remembers that we are not stuck in a particular feeling, but that it will evolve into a new emotional experience in time.

The Research on Expressive Writing and Psychotherapy

When we return to the two modalities of psychotherapy and journaling, it might be clearer now why each has its own advantage in helping us emotionally. Both talking and writing help move emotion through our systems and help us view it with some detachment and time perspective. Researchers have contributed some insight into the relative processes by comparing writing and talking therapies and examining what happens when they are combined.

The beginning of research on emotionally expressive writing was in Dr. James W. Pennebaker's lab in the late 1980s. Two points about this research are particularly relevant to the comparison of the modalities of psychotherapy and journaling for emotional balance. First, his research was originally focused on the topic of catharsis. The whole idea of using writing was an expedient replacement for the examination of catharsis in therapy, as lab space and therapists were in short supply (Pennebaker 1990). The original study of expressive writing already had a comparison to psychotherapy in the background. There was recognition that the two modes of release had a lot in common.

The second significant point about the Pennebaker paradigm, which became a standard for research on expressive writing, was that the explicit instructions were to write our "deepest thoughts and feelings" about an extremely upsetting event (Pennebaker 1990). One of the control groups wrote about trivial topics and the other wrote about the upsetting event in a strictly factual manner. The test group, writing about "deepest thoughts and feelings," demonstrated better outcomes, suggesting that the most beneficial expressive writing includes integration of both facts and feelings.

The specific branch of this research that compared modalities of emotional expression also started in the late 1980s. Edward Murray's lab compared short episodes of outpatient psychotherapy to the Pennebaker paradigm of expressive writing (Murray et al. 1989). At first, they found that two thirty-minute sessions of psychotherapy two days apart were more effective in decreasing negative feelings at later follow-up and increasing positive cognitive changes than expressive writing exercises of the same length. With four sessions, they found the benefits to be equal for both groups, but those who wrote experienced more negative affect immediately following the writing sessions (Donnelly and Murray 1991).

To separate the effects of the interaction from mere vocalization, Murray and Segal (1994) then designed a study with four groups. Two groups described traumatic events, one on paper and one to a tape recorder alone in a room. Two parallel groups did the same thing describing trivial events. The group that did emotional expression, as is common in this literature, showed decreased negative feeling and increases in self-esteem ratings and adaptive cognitions, by self-report. The interesting thing is that the tape and writing group showed no significant differences, and both showed the spike of negative affect immediately following emotional expression. (As an aside, vocalizers used more emotional words and in twenty minutes used about three times the number of words as writers.) The conclusion here is that, again, emotionally expressive writing is powerfully healing and that the simple act of vocalizing did not cause a disappearance of the immediate negative affect.

The researchers concluded that a therapist's presence, therefore, is the variable that prevents the immediate surge of negative feeling after writing. Pennebaker (1990) has also noted that it is normal to feel worse instead of better immediately after expressive writing but that the immediate feelings will typically dissipate on their own within some hours.

A few studies have looked directly at the best of all worlds, combining psychotherapy and written emotional expression. Traditionally the role of writing in therapy has been in the domain of cognitive-behavioral therapy; writing is used for self-monitoring of thoughts and behaviors. Luciano L'Abate (1991) has experimented for years with combinations of workbooks and therapy. He found a workbook for depression had significant but only short-term effect. An anxiety workbook was compared with an assignment of thirty minutes' unstructured writing about anxiety between sessions, and a nonwriting control group. This study showed more long-term benefits in both writing groups, as opposed to the controls who were treated for anxiety without any writing between sessions.

L'Abate went on to design a diverse and large series of workbooks to augment therapy processes, including relational treatments.[2] A 2004 study by Gordon, Baucom, and Snyder concurred that outside writing that was reviewed with the therapist was beneficial to couples recovering from issues of infidelity.

A dissertation study looked directly at the initial phase of psychotherapy combined with the Pennebaker paradigm (Graf 2004). In this study, clients had writing assignments between sessions, about either traumatic or trivial events. Again, the emotional expression group showed decreased anxiety and depression symptoms, and increased interpersonal and social role functioning. They also rated themselves as more satisfied with therapy than the other writing group and were seen by the therapists to be more insightful. The writing clearly boosted the therapy. An interesting side note on this study is that there was no attrition in a sample of forty-four people. This is unusual, both in research and in early psychotherapy process. We might hypothesize that the writing helped sustain people's interest in the process of the psychotherapy.

Smyth and Greenberg (2000) suggest that writing in therapy can help pace the treatment. Difficult topics may be more easily addressed initially and during periods of intensity of affect. Writing may also reinforce gains made in therapy, articulating new levels of insight, adaptation, or cognitive schema.

Writing as a Therapeutic Tool

Desensitization, narrative organization, and positive strategy and imagery building are three mechanisms of action where the two means of emotional management, psychotherapy and expressive writing, seem to overlap.

Desensitization occurs because, in both therapy and writing, the traumatic stimuli are reexperienced in a safe and self-controlled way. This derives from Pennebaker's (1990) original model of catharsis and his observation of the decrease in physiological arousal when emotional tension is released. Research has confirmed that people who write in the Pennebaker paradigm experience objective and subjective measures of decreased arousal, and that the decreases relate to positive improvements from writing. For instance, decreases in salivary levels of cortisol, a stress hormone, is correlated with subjective experience of emotional release through expressive writing. The decreases in cortisol and in emotional acuity seem to occur together, relate to lowered depressive and posttraumatic stress symptoms, and fewer physical complaints (Sloan and Marx 2004).

Narrative organization is also an important principle in the emotional benefits of both writing and psychotherapy. The structures of story and communication transform chaotic and traumatic sensory impressions into contained long-term memory. This containment makes traumatic reactions less easily evoked (Smyth, True, and Souto 2001). Research again backs up the idea, which nearly every fiction reader knows, that story helps us organize and understand our feelings and create an internal space where they can rest more easily.

Pennebaker's continuing research supports this idea. He has analyzed linguistic and usage patterns associated with improvement in emotionally expressive writing. One finding was that a change over time in the number of causal or insight words used related to emotional improvements (Campbell and Pennebaker 2003). Another research group found that expressive writers benefited from instructions to write about specific ways they understand their traumatic experiences (Ullrich and Lutgendorf 2002). These findings further suggest that structure and narrative are building a meta-awareness or perspective that helps balance emotions.

Finally, in both psychotherapy and expressive writing, people can build positive imagery and find silver linings in difficult experiences. Burton and King (2004) asked people to focus on positive experience and self-images in emotional writing and found those exercises to relate to positive mood improvements. This positive aspect of emotional expression, in any forum, is more than just wishful thinking. Articulating the whole range of experience gives voice to positive direction and mentally rehearses its possibility. This is brain training and redirecting of energy that can be extremely productive, if it is done carefully and without denying any of the associated negative feelings.

Although they have all this in common, there are also different things that psychotherapy and personal writing contribute to developing a calmer and more comfortable emotional state. In therapy, someone verbally communicates feelings so that another person understands and receives this message. The immediate sense of having important emotion solidly received is a soothing, healing event that cannot be approximated in a journal. This may be why the research studies showed that the immediate negative affect experienced right after writing did not occur when people shared their traumatic experiences with a therapist.

In writing, emotion is released; in a therapeutic interaction, emotion releases and lands within another person, the therapist. Perhaps this seals up the negative emotion in a felt way. Perhaps the reassuring response of the therapy also has a "recency effect," meaning that the positive impact is experienced last in the situation and is therefore carried away from it.

The therapeutic sharing experience often repairs contrary histories of feelings being dismissed, misunderstood, or rejected. The interpersonal dynamic of therapy returns us to the way we learned about emotion in the first place, from interactions with others, and when those interactions are receptive and accepting, there is a distinct sense of relief that overrides momentary negative affect. As Judith Rabinor (2002) sums it up, "Therapy is about being listened to by someone who nourishes and nurtures the soul. Writing offers another kind of healing experience—a sustained self-listening" (176).

The Journal as Transitional Space

Journaling does bring us a sense of the self in its own domain and encourages a kind of ownership and responsibility for our own process that is unique to the medium. Journaling occurs in an intermediate zone between the inner world of our experiences and the outer world of the paper or screen through which our thoughts pass and become objects. This complex, fruitful zone of the self was termed "transitional space" by D. W. Winnicott (1975), the brilliant pediatrician and psychoanalyst of the mid-twentieth century.

Winnicott saw transitional phenomena as events that occur developmentally, as infants learn the limits of control they have over external events.

Transitional activities diffuse over time into a part of experience that exists between our inner world and consensual reality. These activities form the basis of play and creativity throughout life. They clearly form the basis of journaling, and the journal itself becomes a transitional object, as the worn-out blanket might be for the toddler. Maybe some of the soothing quality of looking over a journal or entry derives from that old sense of comfort in transitional objects.

The journal in this way becomes a place of building a secure but permeable interpersonal boundary. Nothing defines the parameters of our own reactions like the actual screen or page filled with our own words. By leaving expressed feelings in the journal, we also have an automatic aid in containment. And by describing emotions in writing, we practice communicating those feelings. It's a great luxury to edit or ramble in writing, while interpersonal communication is less forgiving.

There is a kind of synthesis of the self that occurs specifically in the activity of writing. It approaches a meditative absorption. Neurologically, huge portions of the brain are involved in the process of converting emotion and thought into symbols and executing movements needed to make those symbols cohere. But the point is more than the brain. There is a convergence of emotion, thought, and physical activity that adds up to more than the parts.

It is a pure experience of process to express oneself without an audience, and in this way journaling is a lot like meditation. Paradoxically, by freezing a moment of the self in writing, the journal writer illustrates the variability of the self, just as the meditator does while sitting still and experiencing all the changes the body and mind go through in time. Both sitting and writing help people see how much the self changes in context and in time, and this leads to a relieving and useful broadening of perspective.

A unique sense of creativity accompanies the expression of emotion and self in the solitude of writing. This was perhaps best summed up by Anais Nin in the preface to *The New Diary*:

> We taught the diary as an exercise in creative will; as an exercise in synthesis; as a means to create a world according to our wishes, not those of others; as a means of creating the self, of giving birth to ourselves. (1978, 9)

It is true that this creative pleasure can be temporary and lonely; what feels like a brilliant flash of insight today can look trite tomorrow, and sometimes it's hard not to share the excitement we found in expressing our feeling in writing. But facing the ownership of our lives and the transience of our emotional experiences is a particular kind of wisdom. Growth and healing are born there in a way that is unique to the personal journal.

Conclusion

Journal writing and psychotherapy are two ways of expressing emotion and building emotional resilience that can augment each other beautifully. Journaling can help people process and solidify psychotherapy gains, particularly at the end of therapy, when the therapist's help is being actively internalized. Therapy is a seam of rich ore for journals, and people often keep journals that trace the changes and developments occurring in the therapeutic interaction. As a general statement, journaling may work better in the sense of managing current emotional processes, where therapy works better to repair historical emotional breaches.

At different times of life, in different situations and for different personality types, one or the other process can be better for helping with emotional balance. Fortunately, we do not have to choose which intervention is best the next time we are emotionally upset. Both psychotherapy and expressive writing exist within a wide universe of pathways to emotional strength and development.

References

Burton, C. M., and L. A. King. 2004. The health benefits of writing about intensely positive experiences. *Journal of Research in Personality* 38:150–63.

Campbell, R. S., and J. W. Pennebaker. 2003. The secret life of pronouns: Flexibility in writing style and physical health. *Psychological Science* 14:60–65.

Donnelly, D. A., and E. J. Murray. 1991. Emotional changes in written essays and therapy interviews. *Journal of Social and Clinical Psychology* 12:334–50.

Frank, A. 2001. *The diary of Anne Frank: The revised critical edition*, edited by D. Barnouw and G. Van der Stroom. New York: Doubleday.

Gordon, K. C., D. H. Baucom, and D. K. Snyder. 2004. An integrative intervention for promoting recovery from extramarital affairs. *Journal of Marital and Family Therapy* 30:213–31.

Graf, M. 2004. *Written emotional disclosure: What are the benefits of expressive writing in psychotherapy?* Thesis submitted to Drexel University, March 2004.

Jacobs, B. 2005. *Writing for emotional balance*. Oakland, CA: New Harbinger.

L'Abate, L. 1991. The use of writing in psychotherapy. *American Journal of Psychotherapy* 45:87–99.

L'Abate, L., and M. G. Harrison. 1992. Treating codependency. In *Handbook of differential treatments for addictions*, edited by L. L'Abate, J. Farrar, and D. Serritella, 286–307. Needham Heights, MA: Allyn and Bacon.

LeDoux, J. 2002. *The synaptic self: How our brains become who we are*. New York: Viking.

Murray, E. J., A. D. Lamnin, and C. S. Carver. 1989. Emotional expression in written essays and psychotherapy. *Journal of Social and Clinical Psychology* 8(4):414–29.

Murray, E. J., and D. L. Segal. 1994. Emotional processing in vocal and written expression of feelings about traumatic experiences. *Journal of Traumatic Stress* 7:391–405.

Nin, A. 1978. Preface to *The new diary*, by T. Rainer. New York: Putnam.

Pennebaker, J. W. 1990. *Opening up: The healing power of expressing emotions*. New York: Guilford.

Rabinor, J. R. 2002. *A starving madness: Tales of hunger, hope and healing in psychotherapy*. Carlsbad, CA: Gurze Books.

Sloan, D. M., and B. P. Marx. 2004. A closer examination of the structured written disclosure paradigm. *Journal of Consulting and Clinical Psychology* 72(2):165–75.

Smyth, J. M., and M. A. Greenberg. 2000. Scriptotherapy: The effects of writing about traumatic events. In *Psychodynamic perspectives on sickness and health*, edited by P. R. Duberstein and J. M. Masling, 121–64. Washington, DC: American Psychological Association.

Smyth, J. M., M. True, and J. Souto. 2001. Effects of writing about traumatic experiences: The necessity for narrative structuring. *Journal of Social and Clinical Psychology* 20(2):161–72.

Ullrich, P. M., and S. K. Lutgendorf. 2002. Journaling about stressful events: Effects of cognitive processing and emotional expression. *Annals of Behavioral Medicine* 24(3):244–50.

Winnicott, D. W. 1975. Transitional objects and transitional phenomena. In *Through paediatrics to psycho-analysis*, 229–42. New York: Basic Books.

Notes

1. A portion of this chapter was first published in *The Museletter*, a publication of The National Association for Poetry Therapy.

2. See the website *mentalhealthhelp.com*.

II

PRACTICE

6

$\mathcal{WOWSA!}$

Play-Based Journal Therapy

CHERIE SPEHAR

Do you know what your play style is?

Do you even remember how to play?

Play is any activity that brings us delight, joy, creative immersion, or/and adventure. Children tend to be fluent in the language of play, but somewhere in adulthood these instinctual responses toward the playful drop away. In fact, the more adults become immersed in "grown-up" lives, the more they tend to forget how to incorporate these playful activities into their lives—or even simply into their self-care practices. This absence of play can lead to apathy, a chronic state of busy-ness, and a subtle refusal of the invitation from the big wide world to engage in its treasures. And for those who face stress or traumatic experiences that add to this dulling of inner light, a paucity of play can affect resilience and recovery time as well.

The aim of this chapter is to introduce the idea of play-based journal therapy, examine its mirrored goals in relation to classic journal therapy, and provide practical tools that therapists, healthcare workers, and facilitators can use to enhance their own practices.

Trauma-Informed Healing

I am both a licensed practitioner and educator in the field of trauma and a registered play therapist-supervisor (RPT-S). Trauma-informed care is a movement across disciplines to acquire and practice with a true and accurate understanding of traumatic stress on the mind and body, and to work synergistically with both in order to maximize healing and eliminate re-traumatizing approaches. The Substance Abuse and Mental Health Services Administration (2014) describes trauma-informed care as a system-wide approach that encompasses six key principles of practice, including

- safety;
- trust and transparency;
- peer support;
- collaboration and mutuality;
- empowerment, voice, and choice; and
- cultural, historical, and gender issues.

Let's together consider some important aspects of being a trauma-informed healer when it comes to play-based journal therapy.

Most of us have walked paths that have left us wounded, fragmented, or at the very least chronically distressed. In fact, many of us have actually experienced traumatic events without realizing the impacts they had on our minds, bodies, and spirits. A basic definition of trauma is most important in understanding the significance of our responses, but even more importantly, how to help.

While there are many societal stereotypes and misperceptions about what trauma is, neuroscience-supported evidence now informs us that trauma is defined as any situation that causes a sense of stress and distress in which the body experiences the fight, flight, or freeze response. The human body responds the same to all overwhelming situations in which the stress response is activated, no matter what type of event it is. For instance, a divorce can be even more traumatizing than witnessing violence or tragedy, if the divorce is perceived as more of a threat or disaster than the witnessed experience.

Thankfully, perceptions of trauma are changing to more accurately reflect this state of overwhelming distress as a potentially traumatic event in our life maps, one that is the basis for ongoing pain, emotional dysregulation, and the classic collection of posttraumatic stress symptoms.

How Does Play-Based Journal Therapy Help?

When we begin a healing process, we seek support for understanding, navigating, and making meaning of

- the experiences of a change event;
- the associated feelings, memories, reactions;
- the experiences of transitions: endings, neutral zone, new beginnings (Bridges 2009);
- the experience of *having* the feelings, memories, reactions;
- the unlocking of private logic/internal belief systems; and
- creating a new narrative.

When working through traumatic stress or painful experiences, the expressive arts are becoming methods and media of choice because of their sensory healing aspects. Because trauma is a sensory experience, not a cognitive one, expressive therapies are highly effective; they work in synergy with the body and bring about active healing processes that engage the parts of the brain where trauma is stored. Of these, journal therapy and play therapy are two of the most consistently accessible and useful modalities.

Play therapy has long been connected to the sensory experience of emotional symbols to release pain, gain insight, reorder traumatic experiences, and develop new neural pathways for making meaning of life events. It is easy to see how play-based interventions promote a deeper engagement in therapeutic process and how they hold transformative powers for health, relationships, personal creativity, innovation, and learning. With journal therapy mirroring these tenets, the combination has an effortless synergistic effect.

Both have expressive properties that parallel each other and form a natural healing bridge between the modalities.

For example, the Association for Play Therapy (APT) defines play therapy as "the systematic use of a theoretical model to establish an interpersonal process wherein trained play therapists use the therapeutic powers of play to help clients prevent or resolve psychosocial difficulties and achieve optimal growth and development."

The definition of journal therapy holds remarkably similar themes. It is defined by Adams (1999) as "the purposeful and intentional use of reflective writing to further mental, physical, emotional, and spiritual health and wellness. It offers an effective means of providing focus and clarity to issues, concerns, conflicts, and confusions."

Here we see a merging of healing themes such as the purposeful and intentional focus on wellness, growth, development, and personal effectiveness. They both aim to find resolution for psychosocial difficulties, concerns, conflicts, and confusions. Finally, both journal therapy and play therapy offer kinesthetic value, which creates sensory catharsis and builds and rebuilds neural pathways.

Additional Benefits of Play-Based Journal Therapy

The Invitation of Softness

Play creates a space that feels warm, safe, and approachable. Adding these elements to the journaling process can deepen, soften, and support the experience on previously untapped sensory levels.

Humor

Often journaling is done to work through painful topics. In play therapy, we know that adding the aspect of fun to promote catharsis is an extraordinary tool in creating an emotionally safe environment to explore tough topics.

Novelty

The brain loves novelty! By introducing unusual, playful, and refreshing ideas into the journaling process, we excite the brain into paying closer attention, and paving new neural pathways that it enjoys traveling. Novelty in the healing journey is a way to increase the firing of new neural connections. We actually grow brain! And the best part is that we "grow brain" in the areas most important for emotional regulation.

Storytelling, Fantasy, and Imagination, Oh My!

Play invites and allows us to go into a world where we can Discover, Explore, Expand, and Pretend (DEEP). When we can go DEEP into our inner core with the mediums of play, we enjoy the parallel process of

- **D**iscovery. The sensory base of play reaches the part of the brain where feelings live without words.
- **E**xploration. Playful journaling creates opportunities to reach parts of self that may have been hidden or are untapped reservoirs of strength, insight, or clarity.
- **E**xpansion. Play-based journaling builds upon, enhances, and expands our use of words. For example, we can then capture the "felt sense" of an emotion, expand our imagination with descriptive writes like Character Sketches (a written portrait of another person, or of an aspect of self) (Adams 1990), or find descriptors that even more closely match the experience we are trying to convey.
- **P**retend. The world of imagination and guided imagery journal techniques are often used as metaphorical approaches to healing. Adding the dimension of a pretend world to the journaling process opens gateways for attending to the previously impossible. It "untames" the journaling process so that inhibitions and limits are relinquished and all realms of mind, body, spirit can be explored. In Pretend World, we also find safety because it offers the chance to be one step removed, providing useful distance.

Mindfulness

Journal therapy is a mindful practice, for it requires a sense of being open, aware, and curious. Likewise, mindfulness itself has been described as a state of playfulness (Goldstein 2012). Because mindfulness practices are quickly becoming a modality of choice for training our brains to respond to stress in healthier ways, combining interventions that inherently promote mindfulness deepens the positive impact on healing and interpersonal effectiveness.

WOWSA! How to Introduce Play

Over the nineteen years of my practice, a synergy began to emerge in which these two passions found a marriage of intent, process, and outcomes. Finally, a more formal conceptualization developed into a playful acronym called WOWSA! (I *know* you want to say it out loud so let's do it, with gusto. Ready? One, two, three—WOWSA! Try it again—even wave your arms around— WOWSA! That's fun, isn't it?)

WOWSA stands for the various ways in which we can add play to journal therapy techniques. It is an acronym that stands for:

- The WAY we write
- What we write ON
- What we write WITH
- The SHAPE in which we write
- What we write ABOUT

W: The *Way* We Write the Words Introduces Play

There are creative *Ways* to form or write the words that become playful. We do this through word movement, artistry, and materials. The *Way* also includes the manner in which we undertake the journal write. By approaching with openness, curiosity, and gentle awareness, we invite the elements of mindfulness and play at once. In this way we can enhance our journaling prompts with artistic and expressive concepts.

O: What We Write *On* Introduces Play

One of the most novel and effective ways to make journaling playful is writing *On* something other than traditional paper. Favorites with my clients include writing on

- wood;
- tissue paper;
- shells;
- rocks;
- popsicle sticks;
- fabric;
- ribbon;
- leaves.

These media can then be turned into art journaling projects, or they can be used for ceremonial purposes. For example, the leaves could float away in a stream, a shell with a personal message could be left on the beach, or written-on ribbon or fabric could be wrapped around a candle.

W: What We Write *With* Introduces Play

Did you know how many tools there are to write *With*? Try these ideas to immediately create a playful environment:

- Use rocks to create marks on paper or the sidewalk.
- Write with sticks in the sand or dirt.
- Make marks on paper with burnt matches and other natural items.
- Use items themselves to form the words, such as several small pebbles arranged in the order of the words of the write.
- Break sticks or twigs into pieces to form words.
- Use calligraphy pens for colorful flourishes.
- Write with feather quills.
- Find pencils made from actual sticks at craft stores.

S: The *Shape* in Which We Write the Words or Form the Letters Introduces Play

In this method, we call to mind the power of visual poetry, sometimes called "shape poems" or "concrete poems."

- Write the *letters* in the condition the word (e.g., upset) is describing:

p e

u s t

- Also consider writing in the font of the word's meaning. For example, when writing about fear, the letters themselves could be drawn as if they are written with a shaking hand.
- A poem or essay can also be written in a shape form, starting with a spiral, a shell, a tree, an ice cream cone, a flower, or many other shapes, and following the outline of the shape when filling in the words.

A: Symbols and Objects to Write *About* Introduce Play

Symbol work in play therapy is a powerful approach to developing insight, clarity, and meaning. To capture what direct words cannot reach, encourage clients to playfully write about a symbol that is an extension of the inner world by introducing metaphors, objects, and element to choose from. Writing about the symbol can inspire access to that which is waiting to be voiced.

WOWSA Interventions[1]

Now let's get to the fun part: *How do we do it?*

Over the years, I've developed more than one hundred play-based journal therapy interventions and more seem to develop each week. Working with age ranges from five and up, the possibilities are fluid, dynamic, and fun. The most exciting part is how my clients, whether little kids, bigger kids, or "big kids" (adults) add their variations to it and create even more richness. Here are few of my favorite creations, well-loved and repeatedly requested by clients of all ages. Ready? Let's play!

Paper Plate Stepping-Stones
(Adapted from the work of Ira Progoff [1992])

Ages: Eight and up

Materials: Any writing utensil, paper plates

Purpose: To identify important life events, assess trauma themes, release emotional energy, add kinesthetic layers to healing story, honor and celebrate life narratives, and/or provide insight and clarity for the life themes and stages impacting life the most in past, present, and future expressions.

WOWSA: Way (movement, artistry), On (paper plates, stones), About (a visual representation and symbol of life milestones)

Steps:

1. Engage the clients in creating their stepping-stones, the life markers that have shaped them in specific ways (Progoff 1992; Adams 1990). It can be done first in the traditional way, as a list of significant life events on paper, or you can begin by having the clients write them on the paper plates right away.
2. If your clients opted to list them on paper first, have them next creatively and artistically transfer them to the paper plates.
3. In a hallway, or a room with enough space, have the clients arrange paper plates on the floor in chronological order. Then, using the following questions to add dimension, depth, and healing openings, invite the clients to move, touch, step on, or otherwise engage with the paper plates.
   a. What do you notice about your stepping-stones?
   b. Are there any you wish were not in your lifeline?
   c. Move the ones you wish you didn't have to step through.
   d. What was the hardest one?
   e. Is there one that brought you joy?
   f. Which ones would you turn over, if you could go back in time?
   g. Which ones were the hardest to walk on or through?
   h. Which stepping-stone is the most meaningful?
   i. Which were the hardest to move on from?
   j. What was it was like to move from this one to this one?
   k. Which were the happiest?
   l. The most slippery?
   m. What would happen if you turned this stone over?
   n. Are there any baby pebbles you would add?
   o. What stepping-stone do you want to get to next?

Store the paper plates in the therapy room so that they can be returned to again and again.

Reflection: As always, you may utilize the Adams (2013) method of post-write reflection (*As I read this, I am surprised by . . .* or *I notice . . .* or *I am curious about . . .*) or consider the following:

- What was it like to complete this activity?
- What was the part of this activity you enjoyed most?
- What was the part that challenged you most?
- What did you experience inside the deepest part of your heart?
- How did you feel before this write/activity? What is different about the way you feel now?

Therapeutic Discussion: Paper Plate Stepping-Stones add a range of playful elements. Not only are we writing ON something that is unexpected, but clients of all ages enjoy the movement and visual representation of their life story. We can tackle tough topics in ways that invite gentle recognition of the impact of life experiences, promote empowerment, and visually demonstrate the power of our passages traveled. This also has the potential to normalize symptoms or provide clarity on the physical expression of stress.

Variations and Advanced Options:

- Use natural rocks and stones instead of paper plates (a favorite of mine!).
- Movement is your friend. Invite client to act out what it felt like to be on a slippery stepping-stone, a happy one. Dance, slide, crawl!
- Create additional baby pebbles with smaller paper plates or stones when working through one of the main stepping-stones. Use the main stepping-stone and set the remaining ones nearby, or around it.
- Create more plates or stones to use as goals, dreams, and wishes.

Fortune Cookie Fun

Ages: Eight and up

Materials: Any writing utensil, fabric fortune cookies found at Training Wheels[2] (or any sort of bag—pouches, organza bags, paper bags), paper quotes cut into strips.

Purpose: To identify important life events, assess trauma themes, release emotional energy, add kinesthetic layers to healing story, honor and celebrate life narratives, and/or provide insight and clarity for those impacting life the most in past, present, and future expressions.

WOWSA: On (novelty paper), Shape (drawing/fonts), About (a unique fortune)

Steps: This activity will require some up-front preparation, but once you do so, it is a playful journal therapy intervention that promises to add benefit and value as you continue.

1. Search, create, write, or paste quotes you love about healing and inspiration (or your theme of choice) into a word document. Use a fun font that is not something a client typically sees. Leave enough space between quotes so that they can be cut into strips.
2. Print the document on playful paper—parchment, vibrant colors, soft pastels—mix it up!
3. After printing, cut the quotes into strips and place one strip into each mystery pouch you have chosen (fabric pouches, organza bags, etc.)
4. Place all of the mystery bags in sight when beginning the session and, when ready to begin, invite the clients to explore them, and pick one that is calling to them. Notice how the fortune cookie/mystery bag feels, and what it looks like.
5. Ask the clients to mindfully jot down a few things about the exterior of the pouch/bag/fortune cookie.
6. Next, invite the clients to capture in five words the feelings they have about seeing what is inside.
7. Using the prompt inside, ask the clients to write any combination of the following:
   a. Read the fortune and take a moment to let it settle into your spirit.
   b. Write about what meaning it may have for you or your life at this time.
   c. How do these words impact your current life stage?
   d. In what way, if any, does this contemplation inspire your movement forward, backward, up, or down?
   e. Draw a picture of the feeling this quote gives you.
   f. Pick one word from this quote that sings to you and give it the words.

Reflection: Invite the client to choose one or more of these reflections:

- What was it like to complete this activity?
- What was the part of this activity you enjoyed most?
- What was the part that challenged you most?
- What did you experience inside the deepest part of your heart?
- Let's explore ways to make the meaning of this quote come alive for you.

Discussion: This is an excellent activity to inspire the mind and playfully encourage exploration and discovery. Because play involves discovery, a "fortune" brings an air of mystery and excitement. Simultaneously, what's inside is also the fuel for the very important work they are doing. Yet, the playfulness makes the walk a little more inviting to take.

Variations and Advanced Options: Creativity is the name of the game here! Use any form of playfulness to establish a sense of fun mystery and anticipation.

- You can tape two small paper cups together to make a vessel with a fortune inside. You may also use upside-down cups and hide something underneath.
- Envelopes—especially decorated ones—make a fun alternative. This is also therapeutic for group work if the client is able to keep the envelope and add artistic claim to his "fortune."
- Tiny boxes found in craft stores are also welcomed by clients.
- For an especially fun variation for writing groups, hide the fortunes in the room by taping under chairs, placing under folders, or in some other way inviting the unexpected.

Word Wide Web

Ages: Ten and up

Materials: Any writing utensil (silver or gold metallic Sharpies recommended), black or blue construction paper, string or fishing line, glue sticks or tacky glue.

Purpose: To explore and discover aspects of internal and external identity, assess trauma themes, identify resources and hurts, recognize resilience and areas for growth and opportunity, and/or assess for areas of resilience.

WOWSA: Way (artistic writing with movement, materials), On (novel paper), With (gold Sharpies), Shape (writing words on and in an unusual shape), About (a metaphor and symbol)

Steps:

1. Introduce clients to the idea that their lives can be very much like a spider web. The spider web functions on a basic structure with named lines,

much like their lives: They have structures, connections, needs, desires, and signals. There are intricate designs, crossroads, connections, and delicate strands. Yet, like the spider web, their lives also hold near miraculous strengths. Like the mysteries of the web, their lives capture promise and discovery.

2. Show clients the outline of a basic web and point out the structural thread lines—Bridge, Frame, Radius, Auxiliary Spiral, Capture Spiral, Signal Line, Anchor Thread.

3. Ask them to consider the symbol of these lines in their own lives:
   a. Bridge (the initial line)—What do I first share with others?
   b. Frame Threads—What are the frames/structures in my life?
   c. Radius Threads—What are the pieces of my world connecting my frames?
   d. Auxiliary Spiral—Write down what I hold inside.
   e. Capture Spiral (the sticky silk)—What do I still need?
   f. Signal Line—How do I ask others for help?
   g. Anchor Thread—What keeps me from falling apart?

4. Invite clients to design their own webs on construction paper, using any combination of materials they choose.

5. As the web is drying, have clients respond to questions from Step 3 on their webs near the lines, using shimmering gold or silver Sharpies.

Reflection:
- What did this write show you about your perceptions?
- What was the part of this activity that taught you the most?
- What part of your Word Wide Web do you feel most protective about?
- What part of your Word Wide Web is strongest?
- What else do you want to capture in your world?
- What do you want to spin in your web so that it is gone?
- What gets tangled in your web?
- In what part of your web do you want to spend the most time?
- What tugs at your web? What do emotional rainstorms do to your web?
- What protects your web most?

Discussion: This is an excellent activity to inspire the mind and playfully encourage exploration and discovery. It also works particularly well with clients who lean toward the scientific, concrete, or logical part of their brains because the metaphor of the spider web is more accessible and sensible to them. The metaphor of the spider web can be "spun" with multiple variations as noted above. For example, how something strong can still be delicate, how something soft can withstand wind and rain (emotional storms).

Variations and Advanced Options:
▪ If time is an issue, print a copy of an illustrated spider web and the client can write the answers within.
▪ You may also suggest that the client draw his or her own web instead of crafting it with other mediums.
▪ Use pulled-apart cotton balls instead of string or fishing line.
▪ Clients may sketch a web, then write their responses to the prompts on the web layout.

Bridges and Sticks

Ages: Eight and up

Materials: Any writing utensil (silver or gold metallic Sharpies suggested), popsicle sticks, cardstock or construction paper (oversized often works best, or taping together smaller sheets), tape, glue. Other drawing mediums optional.

Purpose: To demonstrate movement in the healing process, to visually represent pendulation (the movement between regulation and dysregulation), to capture the process of using sensory regulation skills, to aid in life narrative and meaning making, to honor life transitions.

WOWSA: Way (artistic expression, movement, unique creation), On (popsicle sticks), With (utensils other than pencil), A (using the metaphor of bridge to demonstrate feelings, journeys, stories)

Steps: This intervention is another favorite with my clients. It is helpful at all stages of the healing process and can be used not only to show a transition from one emotional state to another, but on a broader scale, movement from one life stage to another.

1. Mutually determine with the client what aspect of shift, change, transition, or movement they would like to work on, celebrate, or strengthen. Common ideas or prompts might be:

    a. A bridge from where you were to where you are now;

    b. A bridge from where you are now to where you are going;

    c. A bridge from one emotional state to another, such as fear to calm, angry to peaceful;

    d. A healing journey;

    e. Identity shift from Victim, to Survivor, to Thriver.

2. On popsicle sticks the client may then write the words, phrases, sentences, or heart narratives that represent that transition.

3. On paper of the client's choosing, place or glue the sticks into the form of a bridge. Clients will naturally find creative constructs for this; some will be layered with supports underneath, some will be in one single glued line.

Reflection:

- What did this write show you about your journey?
- What was the part of this activity that taught you the most?
- What was the hardest part of your bridge to cross?
- What does your bridge have underneath it?
- What was it like to cross to the other side of your bridge? (Or, if it is some-where they haven't traveled yet: What do you envision the other side might be like?)
- What part of your bridge did you enjoy building the most?
- What is the view from this part of your bridge? From this part?
- Sometimes we walk back and forth across bridges. If you walked back to this side, what would it feel like? If you were standing back at the beginning, how would you be different now? What would look different?
- What would it be like to go back and travel across this bridge with your new wisdom? Is there anything you might have done differently? Would you have built your bridge with the same tools?
- What might I see if I crossed the bridge with you?

Discussion: The metaphor of the bridge is especially helpful when working with clients who sometimes feel stuck. Not only does it help visually demon-strate movement, but it also normalizes the pendulation process in trauma work. Further, this intervention is highly useful for telling life stories and recognizing change. It also invites a client to notice progress and resilience and make meaning of their transformations. Further, Bridges and Sticks can aid in the integration of life experiences and identity. Bridges and Sticks is an intervention that combines multiple parts of the WOWSA Method and can be used for treatment, assessment, closing, and celebration.

Variations and Advanced Options:
- Clients may also glue or place stepping-stones (see rock variation for Paper Plates Stepping-Stones activity) on their Bridge to add dimension and depth.
- Clients may opt to build a 3-D model of their bridge.
- Clients may wish to draw what is under and around their bridge. Remember that this is an area rich with meaning: "Tell me about the water under your bridge," or "I'm wondering what this object is that you drew at the end of your bridge."
- Clients may choose not to glue their sticks to their paper, in order to rearrange the words from time to time; this is especially helpful for stuck places with emotional regulation; it will help a client visually see where the process halts, and perhaps where another piece of the bridge could be added.

Tension and Tangles Tamer

Ages: Eight and up

Materials: Any writing utensil, blank paper of any kind.

Purpose: To demonstrate movement in the healing process, to visually represent pendulation, to capture the process of using sensory regulation skills, to aid in life narrative and meaning making, and/or to honor life transitions.

WOWSA: This intervention emphasizes the Shape element of WOWSA.

Steps:

1. Using the concept of visual journaling, encourage clients to pick something that feels tangled in their lives right now.
2. At the top of the page, using the entire width of the paper, begin the write by overlapping the first several sentences so that they visually create a tangle of words.
3. As the client gradually moves to the bottom of the paper, decrease the width of each line, and reduce the amount of overlapping words. Add vertical and horizontal space to the words.

4. As this happens, remind the client to write about how the knots are being undone, visually representing the transitional state from tangled to smooth, chaos to calm, emotional dysregulation to tranquility.
5. The end of the write should reach the bottom of the page, and consist of only one word representing the opposite of the beginning tangle—the concrete symbol of tension being tamed.

Reflection:
- What did you notice in your body and mind as you completed this write?
- What do you respond to as you gaze upon your creation?
- What energy shifts do you notice in the symbol of your write?
- Tell me about the energy you feel when you look at your Tangle.
- Place your finger on the last word at the bottom of your write. What does it mean to you?
- With your finger on the last word of your write, try closing your eyes and breathing in the calm of that word, releasing any final tensions as you exhale.

Discussion: While a seemingly simple activity, Tension and Tangles Tamer holds such energy that clients ask to return to it often for the regulation process. The visual representation of a tense, stressful, or chaotic state of mind and heart becoming calm or untangled is a powerful mechanism to support a mindful approach to stress reduction. Because we are using a shape and writing in a way that is unusual, this introduces the element of play. It is a unique approach to writing in which clients can exercise their artistic brain hemispheres, while simultaneously empowering themselves to undo their emotional, mental, and physical knots in response to stress. This is also an activity that can be done easily outside of sessions and used as a tool in ongoing practice at home.

Variations and Advanced Options:
- Sometimes it is helpful to begin the write by asking the client to write down one word capturing their state of being in the beginning and ending the write with the same. Notice if there is movement or change.

- Engaging in a meditative or breathing exercise immediately following this write helps support the process of regulation, and can pave a neural pathway of associating this write with relief and positivity.

Inside and Out

Ages: Eight and up

Materials: Black Sharpies, paint (optional), seashells

Purpose: To make space for honoring and recognizing emotions; to address internal and external identity shapers, to access parts of self, to find understanding for how a client engages with self and with the external world.

WOWSA: Way (artistic mediums and movement), On (shells), With (writing utensils that are different from pencils and pens, paint), About (shells provide the symbol with which to write about self)

Steps:

1. Introduce the idea of inside selves and outside selves. Share some information about how there are parts of us we either hide from the world, or no one knows about us, while the external parts of self are how we think the world perceives us, or what we do show to the world, and so on.
2. Have the client write inside the shell the thoughts, feelings, words, ideas, and secrets the world doesn't see, or that the client doesn't want to be seen, or that is held sacred and guarded. *"When in here I feel . . ."*
3. On the outside, the client may write what he wants to show the world, how he perceives himself, his "outer shell" resilience protecting his inner shell vulnerabilities. *"When I'm out here I feel . . ."*
4. Ask the client to show what it is like when the shell is turned upside down so that the interior is exposed, and what it is like for that client when only the exterior is shown to the world.

Reflection:

- What story does your seashell tell?
- Are there parts of your story that you wish others knew?
- What would happen if others knew you felt that way (name something on the inside of the shell)? What would happen if someone in your life knew that about you?

- Shells often get tumbled in the waves. In the same way, we often experience waves—waves of feelings, waves of energy—what kinds of waves tumble your shell? What does your shell feel like?
- What happens when your shell reaches the shore?
- Where does your shell want to be now? Where does it feel most comfortable? On the shore? In the ocean?
- Do you think someday you might need a bigger or smaller shell? What makes you think so?

Discussion: Shells offer multiple opportunities for metaphoric exploration. From the interior/exterior aspect, to where a shell travels, how it arrives, and where the shell most likes to stay, clients can advance their understanding and exploration of self, as well as normalize and integrate these into a healthy identity. This activity accesses several components of WOWSA and introduces natural elements of the world, which inherently hold symbolic value. As well, the process of this write promotes sensory engagement and playfully invites a client to explore difficult issues related to both internal and external distress and pain.

Variations and Advanced Options:
- The client may wish to use more than one shell; the most common variation is using two shells and then closing/opening them to dramatize their emotional expression.
- Use many small shells to write one aspect of internal/external self on each; then, ask the client to arrange and rearrange the shells and discuss what it feels like when one only one part is exposed at a time. For example, "When this one part of you is seen and the rest is hidden, what happens? When all your internal parts are hidden, what external part is seen? What happens if these three parts are showing but the rest are hidden?" The possibilities are endless for gentle exploration with a client.
- As parts of self that once were hidden become strong or a client experiences more confidence in identity, those shells can be altered to demonstrate that movement. It might even be possible for the client to return those to the sea, or other body of water, in symbolic release.
- This activity may also be used with theme variations such as Shadow/Light, External/Internal forces at work, spirituality, secrets, and more.

Caveat

In my presentations about play-based journal therapy, the question occasionally arises about whether a person utilizing these activities is then doing "play therapy." While the techniques shared here are playful, a note should be made that simply introducing the element of play in your work does not imply that you are engaging in play therapy. Just as in journal therapy, play therapy integrity is essential and critical to its success. However, in these cases, the basic framework originates from journal therapy while simultaneously adding an element of play.

Conclusion

Whether you are a life coach, clinician, or facilitator, introducing novelty and play into a healing or insight-seeking process stimulates insight, clarity, and curiosity. This deepens the walk of recovery or growth, and eases the way through the wellness journey. Remember: Our brains love novelty! Brains become excited at the opportunity to learn and experience something new, and by enhancing our work with the therapeutic benefits of play, we extend the opportunity and possibility not only to repave our neural pathways, but to reclaim our very spirits.

May the work you are doing for yourself or with others be inspired by play, and may your interventions continue to capture the WOWSA effect!

References

Adams, K. 1990. *Journal to the self: Twenty-two paths to personal growth.* New York: Warner Books.

———. 1999. A brief history of journal therapy. Accessed January 11, 2015. http://journaltherapy.com/journaltherapy/journal-to-the-self/journal-writing-history.

———. 2013. Expression and reflection: Toward a new paradigm in expressive writing. In *Expressive writing: Foundations of practice*, edited by K. Adams. Lanham, MD: Rowman & Littlefield Education.

Association for Play Therapy. N.d. Why play? Accessed January 11, 2015. http://www.a4pt.org/?page=PTMakesADifference.

Bridges, W. 2009. *Managing transitions: Making the most of change.* Philadelphia: Da Capo Lifelong.

Goldstein, E. 2012. *The now effect: How this moment can change the rest of your life.* New York: Atria Books.

Progoff, I. 1992. *At a journal workshop: Writing to access the power of the unconscious and evoke creative ability.* Los Angeles: J. P. Tarcher.

Substance Abuse and Mental Health Service Administration. 2014. Trauma-informed approach and trauma-specific interventions. Accessed January 11, 2015. http://www.samhsa.gov/nctic/trauma-interventions.

Notes

1. All WOWSA interventions are created by Cherie Spehar.

2. Training Wheels, a creative resource website for teams, groups, or individual clients, can be found at www.training-wheels.com.

7

Therapeutic Writing in Psychiatric Care[1]

CAROL ROSS

Many of us take writing for granted. Although our outpourings may not always be elegantly expressed, we can usually succeed in translating our thoughts into sentences on a page. But consider someone in a psychiatric crisis. A person in acute internal distress can find *thinking* enough of a challenge, without also trying to transfer their thoughts onto paper. This chapter offers insight into how writing has been used effectively in inpatient acute care, as well as psychiatric intensive care.

Medications enable many people with major psychiatric diagnoses to stay out of crisis and out of the hospital for months or years at a time. Just as expressive writing during stable times helps many individuals to stay well, so can writing be therapeutic for someone who is recovering in the hospital from a mental health crisis. However, periods of acute illness often call for different therapeutic writing approaches. Techniques must be both tailored to symptoms and flexible enough to inspire individuals to write whatever they want and need to write at that time.

I facilitate weekly therapeutic writing groups for inpatients in psychiatric wards and a psychiatric intensive care unit. My therapeutic writing toolbox has been influenced both by the work of well-known expressive writing practitioners (Adams 1990; Philips, Linington, and Penman 1999; and Bolton, Field, and Thompson 2006) and researchers such as Laura King (2002) and by the approaches of some mainstream psychological therapies. Much of the writing that takes place in my groups is expressive, descriptive, or creative. Group members often respond very differently to the same exercise. One person may write an imaginative poem, while someone else may write a narrative account of a memory in response to the same prompt.

A typical session lasts an hour and is attended by up to seven self-referred inpatients. A session comprises twenty-five minutes of writing exercises (duration five to fifteen minutes each), and twenty-five minutes of reading aloud and group discussion. The remaining time is taken up with introductions, reassurances, explanations, and evaluation forms. Flexible writing exercises are best, to allow tailoring to individual needs, and give participants some freedom of choice in both the format and content of what they write. See Table 7.1 for details.

The sharing of writing and group discussion is an important element of each session. This is where patients start to reflect on what they have written and discuss their thoughts and insights with the rest of the group. It is wonderful to observe the mutual support that group members give to one another, both in the sessions and subsequently outside the group setting.

Writing, Mindfulness, and Story

Patients will always have their own unique responses to the material offered based on their personalities, styles, preferences, and abilities. With that in mind, there are three specific kinds of writing that are reliably beneficial for acute psychiatric symptoms and diagnoses: journal therapy, mindfulness, and narrative therapy (story).

Adams defines the Journal Ladder as "a continuum of journal therapy techniques, starting with the ones that have the most structure, pacing, and containment, and ending with the ones that have the least" (2013, 45). I use these rungs of the Journal Ladder (Adams 2013):

- *Sentence Stems:* A sentence-completion process (e.g., *Right now I feel . . .*).
- *Captured Moments:* Vignettes capturing the sensations of a particularly meaningful or emotional experience. Written from the senses with strong descriptors.

Table 7.1. Writing Group Facts and Figures

	Acute Care	Intensive Care
Number of beds	27	10
Location	Art and activities room	Open dining area
Frequency/duration	One hour-long session per week	One hour-long session per week
Average patients per session	3	2
Average sessions per patient	2	2
Average length of stay	19 days	20 days
Case mix	The patients in this ward have a variety of psychiatric diagnoses such as personality disorders, schizophrenia, bipolar disorder, and substance abuse. Many are experiencing serious symptoms and behaviors such as self-harm, auditory hallucinations, negative thoughts, anxiety, mania, and psychosis.	The patients in the psychiatric intensive care unit have a similar range of diagnoses to those in the general adult psychiatric ward, but they are usually experiencing more severe symptoms and are judged to be more of a danger to themselves or others.
Typical session	• Introductions • Explanation and reassurances • Five- or ten-minute writing exercise • Reading aloud and discussion • Fifteen-minute writing exercise • Reading aloud and discussion • Evaluation forms • Final ten-minute writing exercise if time allows and patients feel able • Session close	The patients in this unit can find it difficult to sit still and concentrate for more than a few minutes, and they may have low tolerance for other patients. Sessions in the psychiatric intensive care unit therefore often comprise twenty to thirty minutes of writing and discussion with one patient, followed by a similar one-to-one with another patient. Because the sessions take place in an open area, patients, and occasionally staff (e.g., accompanying a patient who needs constant observation), come and go from the writing table freely. Sometimes two or three patients will sit down together to write, but more often there is little or no overlap in the times that individuals spend at the table.

- *Unsent Letters:* A metaphoric communication to another that is written with the specific intention that it will not be shared.
- *Perspectives:* An alteration in point of view (time, space, voice) that provides a different view of an event or situation. (46–47)

Techniques like these help patients work toward therapeutic goals such as broadening of cognitive focus; reframing thoughts, events, and circumstances; developing insight; and improving self-expression.

Expressive writing is made even more powerful when joined with theories and practices from mindfulness-based cognitive therapy (Segal, Williams, and Teasdale 2013) and narrative therapy (Payne 2006). The combination of techniques can help patients attain present-centered effects such as bringing calm, decreasing anxiety, increasing mental clarity, lifting mood, or temporarily shifting the individual's mental focus away from himself and his own problems.

With all psychiatric inpatients, I use writing exercises that have structure and time boundaries, such as short, timed writing bursts inspired by word prompts, or ten- or fifteen-minute timed writes using objects or pictures as inspiration. In psychiatric intensive care I most often use mindful writing, for its calming and focusing effects. With older people with memory problems I use more exercises aimed at eliciting neutral or positive memories in a low-pressure way, such as writing inspired by everyday objects from the past. I use the widest range of exercises in the general adult psychiatric ward, where diagnoses and symptom severity are the most varied.

Six Techniques for Psychiatric Settings

Six of the therapeutic writing techniques I find helpful for acute psychiatric patients, depending on their symptoms, are

- mindful writing;
- fictional characters;

- positive writing;
- perspectives;
- writing inspired by random input and metaphor; and
- creative writing.

Although the techniques are separated below, there is often overlap between them. For example, positive writing can involve writing from an alternative perspective.

Mindful Writing

Writing mindfully means writing nonjudgmentally in and about the present moment. Mindful writing is a sort of writing meditation. Mindfulness meditation is known to be beneficial for well-being and can be used in helping prevent recurrence of depression (Segal, Williams, and Teasdale 2013). Some people find learning to meditate difficult, but find mindful writing easy. Handouts (Ross 2014) are provided to patients on this and other techniques in the hope that they will write a daily journal between the group meetings, and continue after they have left the hospital.

Mindful writing is the technique I use most often in psychiatric units, with all symptoms and diagnoses, because it is calming and relaxing, and can bring the writer out of the world inside his head and into the real world for a time.

Depending on symptoms, I might use exercises like these, starting with the most accessible:

- Choosing and writing about an object or photograph.
- Noticing something in the "outside world" and describing it in detail using as many senses as possible.
- Describing what can be seen, heard, tasted, smelled, and touched in the present-moment environment. *Caveat: Instructions need to be worded carefully in case patients are experiencing hallucinations. For example, if I were to suggest: "write about what you can hear right now" to people experiencing auditory hallucinations, they might write down—and so emphasize—what the voice(s) in their head were saying to them. Instead, I might suggest: "write about the sounds you can hear around you in the room right now."*
- Mindful expressive writing such as writing about how each part of the patient feels physically, starting at the toes and working up, then, if

Matthew

An intelligent young man from a privileged background, Matthew had been using cocaine and other substances before being detained in the psychiatric intensive care unit for several weeks as a result of drug-induced psychosis. When we first met and talked I had no idea that Matthew was experiencing a psychotic episode. In all our conversations, my overall impression was of a well-mannered, educated young man, and a good conversationalist. It was when he read aloud his first piece of writing that I glimpsed the turmoil of his thoughts.

In our first session, a one-to-one, Matthew was asked to choose an object from a selection on the writing table and describe it (mindful writing). He chose a small box in the shape of a country cottage, the roof being the lid of the box. He wrote for fifteen minutes and then read his writing aloud. Rather than a description of the box, Matthew wrote a short story that started with a young man sitting watching television in the cottage, continued with a world war, and ended in post-apocalyptic anarchy. My intention had been that Matthew do some calming mindful descriptive writing but, as sometimes happens, Matthew's mind took over and a dramatic and vivid short story was the result.

In subsequent sessions, when he was recovering from the psychosis, Matthew's writing was always relevant to the exercise, and never again dramatic or shocking. I successfully used a variety of writing exercises with him. In our second session he was joined by a young woman. The prompt was to describe participation in a hobby or activity they have enjoyed, or would like to try (positive writing). Matthew suggested we make this a guessing game, by not directly naming the hobby or activity. It is not uncommon for a very able patient such as Matthew to make suggestions and, provided everyone in the group is capable of taking part, it can work very well, as it did on this occasion.

The two patients read their writing aloud, and we guessed the hobbies/ activities described. This led to a relaxed group discussion that had nothing to do with mental illness and that was unfettered by the confined and artificial environment of the psychiatric intensive care unit.

This small case study offers an example of how therapeutic writing facilitated in a group in a psychiatric unit can both stimulate conversations and facilitate connections between patients. It can also remind individuals of past interests and positive memories at a time when everything looks bleak.

manageable, adding in emotional and mental states. *Caveat: Symptom severity may make this technique not appropriate for patients in psychiatric crisis.*

Perspectives

Writing from another point of view can bring insight and a more helpful perspective.

For example, think about a recent significant event or conversation. Imagine that you are the other person in the conversation or someone outside the room who overheard everything. Write about the event or conversation from this point of view. Now read and reflect on what you have written. When you are finished, note anything that seems to you to be significant or surprising in a "feedback statement" (Thompson 2004, 82).

Here are some more examples of perspectives exercises:

- Write in the past tense, and in the third person about a significant period of your life.
- Write in the first person, present tense, about your past (or future), from the point of view of your past (or future) self.
- Write a letter to yourself from a past/future self or a letter from you to a past/future self.
- Write dialogue between yourself and another person (living, dead, real, or fictional).
- Write in the first person, present tense, as if you were moving through a place such as landscape or a building. The place can be selected from a set of photographs, or remembered, or imagined.

Character Creation Questionnaire

Name of character:

Age:

Appearance (hair, eyes, build, height, etc.):

Voice (quiet/loud? harsh/musical? with/without an accent?):

Personality (outgoing, shy, friendly, suspicious, etc.):

Clothes (tidy/untidy? colors? style? footwear?):

What does this character always carry with him/her?

What beliefs are important to this character? (spiritual beliefs? nationality? culture?):

What are this character's interests? (hobbies? sports? music?):

Where does this character live? (house, cottage, flat, cave, town, countryside, etc.):

Who does this character live with? (family? partner? pets?):

Who is this character's friend (or friends)?

Who is this character's enemy (or enemies)?

What is this character's life's ambition?

What is this character's deepest secret?

What is this character's greatest fear?

What problem does this character have?

What does this character want right now?

Fictional Characters

Creating and writing about a fictional character shifts the mental focus of patients away from themselves and their problems and onto someone else and his or her life.

A variety of prompts can be used to inspire the creation of a fictional character: a selection of personal possessions, a character-creation questionnaire, a box of buttons.

The direction and format of the piece of writing can also be varied. The patient can write about the fictional person's life, about a meeting with him, a

Kenny

A lonely man in his early forties, Kenny was in the hospital because of worsening symptoms of paranoid schizophrenia. He is not an educated man and he does not find writing easy. In the three writing sessions Kenny attended during his time in the hospital, he wrote and said very little. He gave the appearance of being shy and lacking in social confidence. Out of a range of therapeutic writing exercises, the one that really worked for Kenny was the creation of a fictional character inspired by a photograph. Kenny chose a quirky picture of a young woman with her hair dyed scarlet and a magnifying glass held to one eye. He wrote about the young woman as if she were a friend who needed to talk to him about her relationship problems. Kenny really brought her character to life and wrote with empathy about his friendship and support for her.

Reading aloud and discussing participants' writing is an important feature of my groups. On this one occasion, Kenny felt able to share his writing with the group, and he received positive feedback from the other group members as a result. This was the only time I saw him smile.

letter to or from him, about him doing something like a hobby. Here are two examples of this type of exercise:

- Choose from a selection of gloves. Think about who might own the gloves you have chosen. Write about the person wearing or using the gloves.
- Choose from a selection of photographs of people in different situations. Imagine that you know the person. Give her a name, and write a character sketch about her, her personality, where she lives, who she lives with, and what she does.

Positive Writing

People with mental health problems can have a negatively skewed, problem-saturated view of themselves and their stories. Positive writing can open a door and let in some light. Ideally, when a patient goes home from the hospital, she or he can continue to celebrate positives, however small they may be, in the journal every day.

Laura King (2002) proposes that it is not necessary to write about negative emotions or events to gain benefit from writing; in her research studies, people also benefit from writing that inspires happiness or joy. In the hospital, depending on the type and severity of symptoms, I use exercises such as:

- Writing about positive memories, such as happy holidays, times when things went well, exceptions to patients' problem-saturated stories.
- Looking for positives in a current situation, or past experience, and writing about them.
- Writing about neutral or potentially negative topics in a positive way, such as answering questions like: *What is good about this place/rain/winter?*
- Imagining a future where a desired outcome has been achieved, such as recovery from an episode of illness, and writing about it in the present tense, as if the outcome had already come about. This could be in the form of an unsent letter from your future self, addressed either to your present self or to someone who has supported you. Or it could be a present-tense narrative about what the imagined future looks like and how you feel about it.

Caveat: Positive writing should be used with caution with individuals who are entirely negative thinking and/or severely depressed.

Mary

I met sixty-year-old widow Mary while she was recovering from an episode of mania. Mary is bipolar. The first writing exercise of our one-to-one session was intended to be relaxing and calming: writing about photographs of places, in this case postcards of some well-known tourist destinations. I suggested that Mary choose a postcard and describe what she saw in the photograph. I always make it clear that participants are free to write about whatever they wish. Mary selected a postcard of London and chose to write about a memory of a visit there, rather than a description of the picture.

A set of photographs or postcards is a flexible writing inspiration. Someone who is agitated or confused can find writing a description of a photograph of a beautiful landscape or interesting city scene calming; therefore, it is particularly useful as the first exercise in a session. But for some individuals, photographs provoke more personal or emotional writing.

Mary wrote about a visit to London with her mother. Reading the piece of writing aloud led Mary to confide that her mother had passed away the previous day. Sadly, Mary had been too unwell to visit her mother in the hospital, and so had been unable to say goodbye.

With a little encouragement, Mary talked some more, and it became clear that she had happy memories of her mother. I suggested she write about one of those happy memories. She wrote about several memories from her childhood: baking with her mother, picnics, and swimming in the river. Mary smiled as she read and then talked about this longer piece of writing.

We ended the session after this exercise and Mary went straight to find her assigned nurse to share how comforting she had found it writing about her mother, and how amazed she was that she had been able to write and talk about her without crying.

Writing Inspired by Random Input, Shapes, or Metaphor

Writing exercises inspired by random input, shapes, or metaphor often work well with patients who have schizophrenia or who are recovering from an episode of psychosis or mania. Inspiration for this type of writing can include sets of word prompts, story dice bearing symbols or pictograms, and metaphorical questions such as: "If I were a place, what place would I be?" (Bolton 2011, 234) or "What weather are you now?" (Bolton 2012, 38). Again, flexibility is key.

Geometric shapes can be used in a number of ways, including:

- Free writing for two minutes per shape. Prompts could be spoken word prompts, or shapes printed on cards.
- Choosing one out of a set of colored shapes (printed on cards and spread on the writing table) and writing about what the shape means for you and your life at the moment.
- Using each shape in turn, in any order, as inspiration for writing.

Lisa

One cold, rainy day in late fall, a young woman wearing a bright knitted hat came to one of my writing sessions. Lisa was in her early thirties and had been diagnosed with bipolar disorder several years prior to this hospitalization. Although much of the time she is able to stay well on medication and work as a part-time college lecturer, I met her when she was recovering from an episode of depression and was admitted to keep her safe.

Lisa came along to three writing group sessions, one in the ward just before she went home, plus two meetings of a monthly community writing group I lead that is open to all. The following are some of the writing exercises we did together:

- Creating fictional characters inspired by one of a selection of photographs of people and writing about them and their life.

- Writing some dialogue between herself and a fictional character developed using a character-creation questionnaire.
- Writing about the triangle shape.
- Writing about the rain falling outside at the time.
- Writing about what place would you be if you were a (real or imagined) place.
- Writing in response to poems called "Hope" by Emily Dickinson (1999) and Lisel Mueller (1976).

Lisa said that she felt nervous and inhibited about coming to the sessions but found them enjoyable and helpful. She also said she planned to carry on with writing. She particularly liked creating fictional characters, and writing in response to published poems.

One of the benefits Lisa received from the sessions was a reawakening of an interest in writing. I have heard the same comment many times from patients. Individuals who are depressed or otherwise mentally unwell often lose interest in activities that they used to enjoy. Writing can spark a new interest or reawaken a half-forgotten one for some people. This can be an interest in *writing itself*, as it was for Lisa, or an interest in the *topic* being written about.

Creative Writing

When someone is in an episode of entirely negative thinking, such as with severe depression, sometimes the best thing I can do is provide them with distraction, enjoyment, and respite. Creative writing exercises work well. For example:

- The whole group uses the same first few sentences to begin individual stories. Group members share and compare stories.
- Describe an imaginary wooden house. Whose house is it? Who lives there? Is it unoccupied? A vacation home? Where is it located? What might happen there?
- Write a scene from a well-known fairy tale (that has been previously discussed in the group) from the point of view of one of the minor characters.

Anthony

For a couple of months, three patients were regular attenders of the weekly sessions in the general psychiatric ward: Anthony, Linda, and Susan. The patients got along well and enjoyed the writing and sharing of thoughts and ideas that they did together. A very special, but inevitably temporary, group was formed.

We all looked forward to our weekly meetings, but for Anthony, an architect in his late forties, they were the highlight of each week. As well as the burden of being severely depressed and anxious, he had little in common with the other patients in the unit. Before he joined the writing group he spent most of his time alone in his room, trying to read, but lacking the necessary concentration.

Patients teach me how to improve my practice all the time. Anthony taught me that someone can write beautiful prose, but be so severely depressed that almost everything written shifts from neutral or positive to negative within a few lines. When someone like Anthony is in a period of entirely negative thinking, I have found it is best to avoid positive writing, since the writing and thoughts provoked tend to be negative. Instead, I use mostly exercises involving creative writing in some way. The writing exercises below are some of those that worked well for Anthony during his time in hospital:

- Free writing in two-minute bursts using word prompts.
- Collaborative poetry: Each group member contributed three lines for a Kenning about spring. A Kenning is "a metaphorical compound word or phrase (as *swan-road* for *ocean*) used esp. in Old English and Norse poetry" (Mish 2001, 638). We arranged the lines into a poem (Ross 2012, 105).
- Writing in response to published poems: "The House Is Not the Same Since You Left" by Henry Normal (1993), "Wild Geese" by Mary Oliver (1986), "The Road Not Taken" by Robert Frost (1916), and participants' own favorites.

- Writing after a guided visualization that begins with the individual sitting in a garden, and then moving up a mountain, overcoming an obstacle, meeting a friend who gives something useful, and finally talking to a wise stranger at the top of the mountain who proffers a gift and answers one question.

  Anthony said that the weekly writing group gave him respite from his demons, enjoyment, relief from anxiety, and companionship. Joining the writing group coaxed Anthony out of his room and introduced him to some fellow patients with whom he developed the motivation and confidence to converse, both within and outside the group.

- Write about a magic box. What is it made of? What does it look like? Who does it belong to? What (if anything) does the box contain? What are its magical powers? What happens if someone opens the box, or puts something inside it?
- Collaborative poems: Each member of the group composes two or three lines using the same prompt such as *Life is* . . . The facilitator arranges the lines into a poem.

Evaluating the Groups

It is important to evaluate the groups for two reasons: to ensure the writing practice is effective and safe, and to ensure the facilitator receives feedback to inform and develop the methods. I ask patients to complete an evaluation form only if they seem to be well enough, and only if they participated in most of the session. Of patients who attend the general psychiatric ward writing group, 70 percent complete an evaluation form. As might be expected, this is lower, 33 percent, in the psychiatric intensive care unit. This section summarizes two years of evaluations from my groups. Table 7.2 shows aggregate responses and a few representative open-ended statements from acute care patients; Table 7.3 does the same for intensive care patients.

Table 7.2.   Psychiatric Acute Care Patient Evaluations of Writing Group

Patient Evaluations: Acute Care		
This session . . .	*Percent*	*Patient comments to question,* What did you gain from writing group?
Was partly or wholly enjoyable	99	It allowed me to express some of my feelings on paper and in turn helped to detox my mind.
Helped me relax	91	I got to remind myself of just how lucky I was.
Helped relieve my anxiety	90	Helped my mind feel more at ease.
Lifted my mood	92	Took my mind off things in a way.
Helped me understand myself	81	How to express my feelings.
Helped me express myself	90	I can better reflect on my own circumstances.
Helped me talk to others	89	Got my mind thinking of things outside of myself.

One of the main aims in leading the groups is to inspire patients to begin a regular writing practice. Patients are offered an enjoyable writing experience and taught several therapeutic writing techniques. Patients who are engaged in the sessions tend to stay for the whole session, come back in subsequent weeks and in future hospital stays, and encourage other patients to participate. One measure of the effectiveness of the groups is whether these things happen.

Table 7.3.   Psychiatric Intensive Care Patient Evaluations of Writing Group

Patient Evaluations: Intensive Care		
This session . . .	*Percent*	*Patient comments to question,* What did you gain from writing group?
Was partly or wholly enjoyable	100	Understanding about myself.
Helped me relax	91	My old self!
Helped relieve my anxiety	78	Remembering memories that were long forgotten.
Lifted my mood	91	Expressing myself.
Helped me understand myself	85	Looking from another perspective.
Helped me express myself	91	Inspiration, memories, understanding.
Helped me talk to others	79	Writing my thoughts instead of keeping them in my head.

On average, three patients participate in the weekly group in the general psychiatric ward, and two patients participate in the psychiatric intensive care unit. Approximately 60 percent of patients attend only one session, 19 percent attend at least three, and 12 percent attend more than three. It can be a challenge to get psychiatric inpatients to engage with group activities, and the wards consider this to be a very good level of participation. Some of the patients who participate in only one session no doubt only attend out of curiosity or boredom. However, some of the people who come along just to while away an hour of a long day in the hospital are surprised to find how much they get out of the writing and sharing of thoughts, and they come back week after week.

One such reluctant attendee was Susan, who joined the group at the same time as Anthony. She has a diagnosis of emotionally unstable personality disorder and was admitted to the hospital because of a severe depressive episode with psychotic symptoms and risk of self-harm. Prior to coming to the group, Susan was sure that writing would not be for her, but was persuaded to attend by another patient. She enjoyed the first session and this encouraged her to keep coming.

Susan has so far attended seventeen sessions over the course of two hospital stays, as well as two sessions of my open community group after going home. She also started a daily journal while she was in the hospital. In her evaluation Susan noted that the benefits of the group included lifted mood, positivity, relaxation, confidence, a sense of achievement, calming, a reminder of happy memories, and "for the first time in years" something to think about other than her problems.

Conclusion

It can be challenging to inspire psychiatric inpatients to attend and engage with a therapeutic writing group, but it is deeply satisfying and rewarding when success is achieved. As is evidenced in the evaluations, patients report a range of real changes resulting from attending even a few sessions of the writing groups. They leave with concrete tools to extend these benefits into their outpatient lives.

References

Adams, Kathleen. 1990. *Journal to the self.* New York: Warner Books.

——. 2013. The journal ladder. In *Expressive writing: Foundations of practice,* edited by Kathleen Adams. Lanham, MD: Rowman & Littlefield Education.

Bolton, Gillie. 2011. *Write yourself: Creative writing and personal development.* London: Jessica Kingsley.

——. 2012. Write to learn! Not learn to write! In *Words for wellbeing,* edited by C. A. Ross. Penrith, UK: Cumbria Partnership NHS Foundation Trust.

Bolton, Gillie, Victoria Field, and Kate Thompson, eds. 2006. *Writing works: A resource handbook for therapeutic writing workshops and activities.* London: Jessica Kingsley.

Dickinson, Emily. 1999. Hope. In *The poems of Emily Dickinson,* edited by R. W. Franklin. Cambridge, MA: Harvard University Press.

Frost, Robert. 1916. The road not taken. In *Mountain interval.* New York: Henry Holt.

King, Laura A. 2002. Gain without pain? Expressive writing and self-regulation. In *The writing cure: How expressive writing promotes health and emotional well-being,* edited by S. J. Lepore and J. M. Smyth. Washington, DC: American Psychological Association.

Mish, Frederick C. 2001. *Merriam-Webster's collegiate dictionary.* 10th Ed. Springfield, MA: Merriam-Webster.

Mueller, Lisel. 1976. Hope. In *The private life.* Baton Rouge: Louisiana State University Press.

Normal, Henry. 1993. The house is not the same since you left. In *Nude modelling for the afterlife.* Northumberland, UK: Bloodaxe Books.

Oliver, Mary. 1986. Wild geese. In *Dream work.* New York: Atlantic Monthly Press.

Payne, Martyn. 2006. *Narrative therapy: An introduction for counsellors.* 2nd ed. London: Sage.

Philips, Deborah, Liz Linington, and Debra Penman. 1999. *Writing well: Creative writing and mental health.* London: Jessica Kingsley.

Ross, Carol. 2012. Writing together: Therapeutic writing in mental health (chapter 7) and Reflections of a writing practitioner (part 1). In *Words for wellbeing*, edited by C. A. Ross. Penrith, UK: Cumbria Partnership NHS Foundation Trust.

——. 2014. *Words for wellbeing*. Blog: http://trioross.wordpress.com/.

Segal, Zindel V., J. Mark G. Williams, and John D. Teasdale. 2013. *Mindfulness-based cognitive therapy for depression*. 2nd ed. New York: Guilford.

Thompson, Kate. 2004. Journal writing as a therapeutic tool. In *Writing cures: An introductory handbook of writing in counselling and therapy*, edited by G. Bolton, S. Howlett, C. Lago, and J. K. Wright. Hove, UK and New York: Brunner-Routledge.

Note

1. Unless otherwise stated, the individuals mentioned in this chapter were, at the time described, inpatients in a general (acute) adult psychiatric ward. Their names and personal stories have been altered to protect their identities.

Now That I See

Journaling with Deaf Teens

DONNA HOUSTON

Her face was passive, having no discernible expression for a full three minutes. Yet her eyes would not leave the page that was scribbled with lines and words—the first real evidence that her story had not only been "heard" and understood, but now recorded, made real and tangible. When she finally looked at me, the tears started to flow and she said—with her hands—"Show this to my mom so she can know me."

She was seventeen at the time, and though she couldn't have understood many of the words on the page before that day, she understood them clearly in that moment. And she understood her own life experience in a whole new context.

I have worked with high school students in state schools for the deaf for twenty-two years. Starting as a speech pathologist, I earned certification in deaf education and taught in the classroom, and eventually became a professional school counselor. During my fourteen years in counseling, I have found journal techniques to be my most effective tool working with young individuals who are deaf. However, these techniques are often highly modified and to understand why, you must first understand the impact of deafness.

Here I must assert a disclaimer on broad categorizations. The range of literacy, language usage, communication, and self-awareness among deaf and hard-of-hearing individuals varies greatly. The experiences shared here are my experiences with deaf children who are not proficient language users, a common outcome of early-onset loss of hearing. Many deaf people do become extremely adept at literacy and communication.

The degree of literacy among the deaf is affected by many variables: the age at which someone became deaf, the level of hearing loss, cognitive ability, and any secondary disabilities such as learning disabilities or autism. Obviously, if a person has acquired language and literacy prior to becoming deaf, they will probably be a proficient language user. However, if a child is born deaf, or has an early onset of deafness, acquiring language will be challenging.

Most hearing children acquire language prior to entering school, but for a child who had no early language input (either aural or visual), language—and therefore literacy—will be impaired for a lifetime. Surprisingly, the mode of language input (aural or visual) is not as much a determinant as is the consistency of early language input. A child who is born deaf and has deaf parents who communicate fluently in sign language will acquire language normally. The prognosis for literacy does not depend upon which language or modality is used, but upon the consistency of language input at as early an age as possible. Depending upon the type of hearing loss, hearing aids and cochlear implants will help a child acquire language aurally *if used early enough.*

The degree of hearing loss covers a great spectrum: mild to profound, unilateral or bilateral, and many unique compositions of hearing loss. The variations of loss are limitless, and even a small loss in one ear can affect development. Hearing loss is often frequency specific, meaning that a child may hear some speech sounds, but not others. Typical hearing losses affect the high frequencies the most, meaning that the consonants in speech are not heard. Thus, connected speech is perceived as a string of vowel sounds only, making it difficult to understand the meaning of speech.

Even children who have frequent, but temporary, ear infections are often delayed in their language development and need to visit with the speech and language pathologist at school to help them catch up on specific skills that were missed during important stages of language and speech development. If the child's hearing is restored to normal, development continues, but if a loss is permanent, the child may never catch up,

Like most people, I'd always imagined that, if forced to choose, I'd rather be deaf than blind. I changed my mind when I fully understood the impact of childhood deafness. Helen Keller said it succinctly: "Blindness separates me from things—deafness separates me from people" (Love, 1933). Imagine that "separation from people" occurring at birth.

We now know that babies in utero respond to sounds and voices. Newborn babies can actually recognize and respond physiologically to their mother's voice. By hearing speech, babies begin to develop speech. And when a baby begins to mimic speech sounds, adults respond with smiles, coos, reinforcement, and more speech modeling. Bonds are strengthened. Speech is further developed. However, when deafness occurs, this pattern of bonding and reinforced learning breaks down, and two very important aspects of human development are consequently impacted: language/communication, and social/emotional well-being.

Language, Communication, and Literacy

Through listening and speaking, a child's language develops. Vocabulary, grammar, and structure are acquired naturally and continually throughout childhood. No special effort is required. Everyday communication allows him to engage in relationships and activities. Incidental learning occurs everywhere. When a child is a proficient language user, she can then begin to read. Reading is accomplished by matching the orthographic representation of *speech* to words and sentences the child has *heard*. Reading introduces new vocabulary and new concepts. After reading has begun, children start to write, putting the letters and words on paper to match what it *sounds* like to them. Academic learning is dependent on this process.

So, if literacy is based on hearing, and academic learning is based on literacy, what happens when a child is born deaf? The lucky child has parents who ensure communication by any means possible, such as hearing aids, cochlear implants, and sign language. If the hearing loss is such that it can be aided with technology, the process to literacy and academic success continues, depending on how much vocabulary the child misses, how many conversations he doesn't have access to.

However, if for some reason the child is permanently excluded from language input (i.e., the hearing loss is undetected or unresponsive to hearing technology, or the family does not communicate in an accessible language mode), the child will have no access to the normal methods of learning vocabulary and acquiring language. There will be no participation in family or peer conversations. There will be no socialization in which to learn appropriate communication strategies. It is no wonder they arrive at school with a deficit in basic concepts and vocabulary.

In general, children who are born deaf or acquire deafness in childhood are very often language-deficient, having low vocabulary and reading, writing, and academic skills. Not only that, but language-deficient brains work differently. Short-term memory and retention are often affected. The detrimental impact of language impairment on the life of a deaf person cannot be overstated.

Social/Emotional

As Helen Keller implied, separation from people is the most devastating aspect of deafness. Family and social relationships are impacted from birth. Although some families learn sign language, many do not, or perhaps only one member of the family does. It is hard to imagine, but I have actually had high school students who did not know their parents' and siblings' names—not even a particular sign or gesture to refer to members of the family. As the child grows, normal peer interaction is impaired because of communication and educational issues. Many of my students arrive in high school with little self-awareness and poor social skills. Because deafness is a low-incidence disability, there are very few counselors or psychologists who can sign or understand the issues of deafness. The majority of deaf and hard-of-hearing students in the United States are taught with hearing peers, usually with the assistance of a sign language interpreter who signs the educational content of their classes. Direct peer communication is limited. Fellow classmates often learn some signs, but as they develop into adolescence, the deaf child can feel increasingly isolated. At a time of life when self-image is developing, she can see with increasing clarity that she is different, and unable to be a part of what is so important to every adolescent—a group of peers with whom she can identify. The deaf child lacks the conversational skills that come from communicating across categories of people (adults, peers, teachers, parents, friends).

If there is plenty of accessible communication at home with parents and siblings, the feelings of inadequacy and isolation are mitigated. All too often, however, the deaf child also has no one at home with whom he can fluently and deeply communicate. Thus, he enters the adolescent years with multiple deficits. In addition to a low language, vocabulary, and concept base, he lacks basic conversation and social skills. Some have learned to talk only with adults, something I frequently see with students who've spent their developmental years communicating only with interpreters. By the time they are teens very often they are socially immature and do not know how to relate to their peers, even though they desperately want to. Sadly, often they don't even recognize that they want to. These kids don't have the internal language structures for self-analysis or the external input to help them see themselves more clearly. Depression is common.

Experiences with Journaling

In 2011, I attended a conference on journal therapy taught by Kathleen Adams. I was attracted by the statement in the brochure that promised effective techniques to use with clients with limited language or cognition. I learned about the Journal Ladder (Adams 2006), a continuum of techniques that ranges from concrete to abstract and from contained and structured to free-form. I knew journaling was an effective tool for personal change, but I did not know how it could be used for students who struggled with vocabulary and language.

Many of my students communicate using sign language. American Sign Language (ASL) is a visual/spatial, full-fledged language with a grammar and syntax all its own. It does not follow English grammar. Often deaf children write in ASL word order, which can be confusing to English language readers. My students aren't just uncomfortable with writing; they are students who don't know what the English language sounds like and are unable to put the words they know into anything that resembles an English sentence. How can they learn to write when they do not read and understand written English?

When they do write, there is often no logical word order or correctly spelled, recognizable words. The meaning is often impossible for a reader to derive out of context. These students know that past attempts at writing have been met with confused expressions and baffled responses. They have experienced humiliation and frustration as a result of their writing attempts. To say that they are terrified and resistant to any type of unstructured writing assignment is an understatement.

So, how to get them journaling? Simple: I do the writing for them. As with anyone's personal journal, there are no rules, no worrying about form or sentences or grammar. I just focus on the words and phrases that represent what they are signing to me, at least in the initial stage. Later, if we are going to present the writing to someone, say in a letter, the English teacher in me comes out and we work together to draft some simple English, simple enough that the student can read—yes, *read*—the letter and know what it contains. This takes practice, which not only leads to learning of new vocabulary and English structure, but also to more processing of the meaning and the message that has been communicated.

Visual-Spatial Journaling: Charts, Graphs, and Icons

Because ASL is a visual-spatial language, our journaling often takes that form—visual and spatial. I have found that drawing, graphing, and labeling is more effective than writing sentences. After a good model of their particular situation is on paper using symbols and labels, students regularly stop in to mark their progress on various scales that chart many facets of themselves, including emotional well-being, social, and school related issues. It gives language-deficient kids a way to reference and communicate without the vocabulary and structure that is so elusive to them, while at the same time helping them learn the essential concepts and vocabulary of self-awareness.

There is no emphasis on learning the words. Because this is all about them, and generated by them, there is an inherent interest in learning the words. To my great delight, students eventually start using the words themselves.

When students start to tell me their story, I get out a very large piece of paper and start to write key points. This is the hook, and it is extremely powerful. The moment a student sees his thoughts recorded on paper, something changes; he becomes completely focused on that piece of paper, and thoughts and ideas come pouring out. As the student talks (signs), my job is to help clarify and organize.

I cannot stress how important clarification and organization is for students with impaired or delayed language. Without a strong internal language system, it is very difficult to organize one's own thinking. Concepts such as *first/ second, if/then, before/after*, and *because* are *language based*, as are the concepts of future and past tenses. Without internalizing those language structures, students have not had a way to analyze or explore events, sequences, and relationships in their lives, much less express them.

I usually have to ask many questions to get the story clear. By that time there is a long horizontal line drawn on the page representing a specified time frame, and we are charting the who, when, where, and what (all language-based concepts, which not all students understand) of the story. Sometimes that story is their whole life.

For students who are depressed, we go back looking for a time when they were happy and record the circumstances of their lives at that time. Visual prompts are usually needed, including a chart containing the caricatures of faces in various states of emotion. These kids don't have the vocabulary to express emotion, but they can identify feelings in pictures. Thus, we develop a scale of emotional well-being, with happier faces progressing upward, and sadder faces progressing down on the scale, corresponding to the numbers one through seven. This becomes the X-axis of our drawing.

The Y-axis represents time. This timescale can be marked in various ways: If we are looking at a long-term problem such as depression, it is usually marked by their age. If we are looking at more immediate problems, the time line can represent the current school year. If we are sorting out recent peer problems, the time scale may be shorter. The line moves forward in time and either up or down on the scale of emotional well-being, thus visually demonstrating significant events and catalysts. Students begin to associate their feelings with events and most significantly, their actions.

Once the graphing is done, I don't usually have to tell students what conclusions to draw; they can see it for themselves. We then write about it in the student's journal. This is where the student tells me her story, and I translate it into written English. It is this process that seems to transform them. This is the product of which they are so proud. They act as if this is a formal, legal document that suddenly legitimizes their experience.

When writing for students, I always promise confidentiality (with the usual caveats) but more often than not, students want these writings to be shared with parents, teachers, peers, and even the principal. It is about them; what has been so difficult to communicate with others can now be shared.

The following story is a case in point, an example of the power of the written word for kids who do not write. Lilly, a usually happy sixteen-year-old girl, came to see me saying she was very sad and depressed. She couldn't focus. She said she didn't want to be in school anymore, but did not know why. When I asked how long she'd been feeling this way, she didn't really know.

I got out pencil and paper and drew a scale of one to ten, asking her to rate her emotional state as of that moment. I then asked her to mark where she was three days before, and a week before, and so on, until we identified the time *just before* the emotional downturn.

From that point, we drew a time line and started to write down events that occurred and the corresponding number on the emotional scale. We eventually pinpointed the evening she had begun to feel so sad. She had felt fine at basketball practice, and at dinner. Then she watched some TV and went to bed. She remembered having bad dreams that night having something to do with the news story she'd seen that evening; the actor Heath Ledger had died from a drug overdose. As she talked, it became apparent this had impacted her deeply. She explained that she'd always felt close to him because she had identified with him in some way. Clearly, she was disturbed by his death and didn't know how to process this loss.

After talking about it, she decided we could write him a letter telling him how she felt, and how sad she was to lose him. Lilly was a student whose background with deafness had led to severe language deficits so as she signed, I wrote, and her feelings poured onto the page in words she'd never seen before, but was learning now. When following up with Lilly in the subsequent days, she consistently rated her emotional state at a high level.

Scales, Maps, and Clusters

One of my favorite charts is one I use frequently to help students gauge their emotional state and social adjustment. There are four distinct lines, each representing a year in high school, labeled nine, ten, eleven, and twelve. Starting with the ninth grade, the first line is extremely wavy with steep ups and downs, representing emotional and social turmoil. The visual map seems to help students instinctively understand the turbulent emotions and changes. Each successive year shows the lines becoming slightly smoother, the ups and downs more spread out and less intense.

I relate these changes to adolescence, including changes in body and brain, and how, over high school, they mature physically, intellectually, emotionally, and socially. This helps to "normalize" students in crisis, letting them know that their social and emotional upheaval is common to all, and that it eventually does get easier. I sometimes refer to this as the "scale of maturity." Year after year, my students testify to its accuracy. Students will show me where on the scale they are at the moment, which opens the door to discussion.

One of the appeals of this charting is that students begin to see that they are a part of something universal, a normal teenager, like others their age. I often bring the seniors in to talk about the scale with younger students, and it is always enlightening and reassuring. This is then something we can write a summary paragraph about. Again, putting the words and concepts on paper seems to somehow make it "real" for the students.

Another technique I use is known in the world of deaf education as visual mapping or cognitive mapping and is referred to in Adams's work as Clustering (1990). I often use this technique when helping students sort out the social and family network of their lives.

A circle is drawn and labeled in the middle of the page. From the central idea or topic, thoughts and associations spin off in additional circles connected to the central thought by a line. This continues as a chain, creating a free-associative map.

In the classroom, the label is the topic to be analyzed, and outlying branches contain various aspects of that topic. It is a good format for brainstorming and for helping deaf kids "see" the many things that are related to the topic. I use this format in guidance counseling to discuss post-secondary life, with the center circle representing a specific job, and the outer circles representing the various paths to get there, or to other aspects of a successful life. Often, however, the topic—or central circle—represents the student himself. This allows us to then look at relationships with others: family, school, friends, counselor. The following story of a male student named Chris illustrates this technique.

Chris came to see me frequently because, in his perception, other students constantly were cruel and rejected him. In our small, Midwestern deaf school, Chris was a student who dressed quite outside the norm, wearing dark eyeliner, dark lipstick and nail polish, and tight gothic-style clothing. He was also immature and pestered other students relentlessly with startling behavior. Chris could not see how his own behaviors contributed in any way to his social isolation. I really struggled with how to make it clear and visual to Chris that he had a part in this drama—that he was not totally an innocent victim.

I drew a large circle that represented the student body, with dozens of small circles inside that represented individuals. We discussed what unified the students within that circle and Chris immediately drew himself as a small circle outside of the larger circle. We discussed what changes he would have to make if he wanted to (a) be within that circle, or (b) avoid being hurt by criticisms from those within the circle. We discussed that there was nothing wrong with choosing to be outside the circle, but that he couldn't expect others to behave as if he were inside of the circle.

Chris decided he did not want to be within the circle, but he began to understand quickly that he was not powerless; rather, he was making choices. Through our journaling together, he learned to be more respectful of others, regardless of their position in or out of the circle. Chris went through years of making decisions, good and bad, that affected his proximity to the "norm" circle. At times he was fully within it. He became adept at charting his location on the "map," explaining his choices and how they influenced his position. At graduation, Chris proudly claimed his journal and took it with him.

Conclusion

With each and every chart, map, drawing, or scale, there are words and labels. These words are not part of a vocabulary lesson; they are words that describe students' lives. The words are intrinsically important to the students. When I follow up with language-impaired students, I encourage them to do their own journaling in the form of pictures, charting, and drawing. They come back to me with a description of their week in the form of pictures (real and drawn), or marks charting one aspect or another of their lives. I provide captions and words, but often I find they are attempting these themselves already. Sometimes they have already written their story in various degrees of English sentences.

The most important thing I have learned in this process is that there is great power in recording oneself on paper. Listening to my students and conversing with them is fine, but it is nothing compared with the magic of organizing their random thoughts and putting them on a page. It is *absolutely* the most powerful thing I can do for them and they usually cannot take their eyes off the page. It makes thoughts that were disorganized and overpowering become tangible and manageable. In other words, it gives deaf students the power of the journal. We all have a need to be heard, but more importantly we need concrete evidence that our journey is not just ephemeral, but real, recognized, and documented.

References

Adams, Kathleen. 1990. *Journal to the self: Twenty-two paths to personal growth.* New York: Warner Books.

———. 2006. *Journal therapy: Writing as a therapeutic tool: A training workbook.* Brentwood, TN: Cross Country Education.

Love, James Kerr (ed.). 1933. *Helen Keller in Scotland: A personal record written by herself.* London: Methuen.

9

Roots of Resilience

Writing for Practitioner Self-Care

SUSAN SMITH PIERCE

Resilience is the ability to bounce back after a setback, to get up and go on. It can be developed and built in conscious ways through mindful self-care. Many of us who work as practitioners in the helping professions do a very good job of nurturing others' self-care and resilience, while sometimes neglecting to do the same for ourselves.

Think back to the last twenty-four hours: What have you done to recharge and renew yourself? How do you consciously seek to build your own resilience?

A self-care practice that includes regular check-ins with thoughts, feelings, priorities, stresses, goals, work habits, and other personal and professional management matters is important if we are to stay healthy, happy, and functioning throughout the life of a career. We know that journal writing is an immediate, effective, accessible, and useful stress management practice. What we perhaps haven't fully appreciated is the role our journals can play in building resilience and activating our coping strengths.

I am the director of professional development and training for Southwest Family Guidance Center and Institute, a mental health agency with six locations throughout New Mexico. The center was founded in Albuquerque in 2004. I coordinate and conduct regular trainings on treatment modalities and interventions for various client groups, best-practice standards for treatment of specific diagnoses, and ethical considerations in mental health. In addition, I direct the center's internship program, which attracts large numbers

Resilience is . . .

Resilience is like the wind. Going with the flow, sometimes you have to pick up speed and sometimes you have to stop. You don't want to take things too personally. You need to just let things go through you.

—*Danielle, child/family therapist, clinical supervisor*

of master's and doctoral level students from a wide range of counseling and social work programs.

As you might imagine, I work with large numbers of practitioners. I can validate that almost without exception, each of them scrambles to juggle client schedules, supervision, continuing education, agency or private practice, raising kids, two-career or single-parent households, and the list goes on. It's no wonder that self-care, if it appears at all, is seldom near the top of the list. That's why I've prioritized including journal writing and resilience training in my work with interns and supervisees, helping them explore six qualities that I have identified as significant for resilience: social support, proactivity, empathy, gratitude, realistic optimism, and spirituality.

Expressive Writing, Neuropsychology, and Resilience

Resilience is built one day at a time. When our lives are characterized by personal strength, meaning, purpose, and feelings of genuine pleasure, we embody resilience (Buckwalter 2011). Expressive writing provides a pathway to our deepest thoughts and feelings. It enables us to process and regulate our emotional responses. It connects us to our resilient self—the self that cultivates these key characteristics of resilience.

There is a substantial body of literature that supports the beneficial effects of expressive writing on physical health and cognitive functioning, two conditions that support resilience. Three decades ago psychologist James Pennebaker conducted the landmark study in which participants were instructed to write their deepest feelings about the most traumatic experience in their lives for four consecutive days, twenty minutes a day. The results were improved physical health as evidenced by fewer doctor visits and increased overall sense of well-being (Pennebaker and Beall 1986).

King and Miner (2000) found that expressive writing might promote resilience-building self-regulatory processes that would lead to health benefits even in the absence of instructions to experience or reexperience intense negative emotions. Participants in the study wrote about the positive outcomes ("silver lining") of a traumatic event. This produced the same health benefits as writing in the classic trauma-based model, without any negative outcomes. Instead, they found that participants were able to self-regulate, confront, control, and structure their thoughts and feelings about the traumatic event, as well as proactively (and often with gratitude and even empathy) identifying outcomes they regarded as positive, such as discovering inner resourcefulness.

King (2001) found that writing about life goals and a person's best possible future self (in our language, perhaps invoking the resilience factors of realistic optimism, proactivity, and probably social support) was associated with decreased illness and a significant increase in subjective well-being.

Other researchers found that it can be helpful to write about current difficulties such as those associated with workplace injustice (Barclay and Skarlicki 2009) or anger felt by sufferers of chronic pain (Graham et al. 2008). Writing about future stressful events such as an impending graduate entrance exam (Dalton and Glenwick 2009) also produced positive results in decreasing rumination and worry. These studies signal the wide range of issues that, when written about in an intentional way, can call forth moments and situations that activate our resilience muscles.

The ability to bounce back rather than get stuck during times of adversity depends on learned patterns of response to other people and events. These become fixed from an early age. Neuroscience has come to understand how to rewire neural circuits in the brain and rebuild the brain's functioning to increase resilience. Research suggests that it is the internal response of

How's Your Resilience?

By Robin Troncoso, MA, LMHC (2013)
Southwest Family Guidance Center, Albuquerque, New Mexico
Score yourself by ranking the following statements on a scale of A (not often), B (sometimes), or C (much of the time).

1. I practice the self-care measures that I teach my clients. _____
2. I experience pervasive fatigue, anxiety, or/and feelings of being overwhelmed. _____
3. There are days when I feel exhausted and drained by my clients, family, and friends. _____
4. I fall asleep easily. My sleep doesn't seem to be interrupted by any workplace stress or concerns I may be experiencing. _____
5. I prioritize my own self-care and give myself the breaks, rest, and leisure that I need. _____
6. My close family members or friends express concern that I am not taking care of myself. _____
7. Feelings of resentment, being overwhelmed, or exhaustion prevent me from being present to family and friends in the way I want to be.

    _____

Give yourself the following points:
For statements 1, 4, and 5: A = 1, B = 2, C = 3
For statements 2, 3, 6, and 7: A = 3, B = 2, C = 1
Your total score: _____
If you scored 18-21: Congratulations! It sounds like you've got good resilience habits.
If you scored 13-17: You've got some good practices in place at least some of the time, but you may be susceptible to workplace stress.
If you scored 7-12: Take a deep breath, keep reading, and see if you can put some simple self-care practices into place as soon as possible.

resilience, no matter what the external trigger, that is important for positive neurological change (Graham 2013). Writing is one of the ways that resilience habits can be installed (see D. Ross, chapter 2).

"Simply put, expressive writing can help us process emotions and re-organize our brains" (Pierce 2014).

Qualities of Resilience

Resilience encompasses skills, attributes, and abilities that enable individuals to adapt well to hardships, difficulties, and challenges. A rubber band is resilient: Stretched to its breaking point, it has the flexibility to resume its original size and shape. Flexibility and active effort are fundamental building blocks to resilience.

Those who work as helping professionals have honed their skills to nurture and care for others in times of extreme stress and adversity. Ironically, these same helping professionals frequently overlook their own stress and adversity in the service of others, and they don't always practice the coping strategies they teach to their clients and patients. The qualities that boost resilience are an essential part of physical health and well-being. It may also be that self-care is an integral part of professional ethics; maintenance of high standards of practice requires resilience.

Resilient people have strong social connections. They are proactive, realistically optimistic, empathic, grateful, and spiritual. They feel a sense of being part of a larger whole that connects them to meaning and purpose.

Resilient people take responsibility for their own self-care. Skovholt and Trotter-Mathison offer a way to check in on your resilience:

> Try identifying a time when you made the decision to act in your own behalf instead of waiting for someone else to do this for you. How did you feel? What were you thinking? At that point, whether you realized it or not, you were making an active contribution to the development of your resilient self. (2011, 167)

To extend this check-in, set your timer for ten minutes and write the story of this experience, either by hand or on keyboard. You'll likely find layers of insight and an increased understanding of your own roots of resilience.

Writing Prompts

Choose from the questions below to begin exploring the roots of your own resilience. Begin with five minutes for each question, and add to it if you wish.

- What is your personal definition of resilience?
- What do you consider to be the most essential qualities of your own resilience?
- What is the current state of your resilience?
- What stops you from being more resilient?
- Think about someone who embodies resilience for you. Write a character sketch (a written portrait or description) of this person's inner and outer qualities.

When you have finished this write (and all of the writes for this chapter), reread what you've written and write a sentence or two of reflection. This reflective process is a key component in developing insight and actionable wisdom (Adams 2013).

Reflections

As I read this, I notice a tenderness in my heart (reflection following write on gratitude).

My spiritual journey is at the core of who I am. For years my time in the pine forest carried me, and I feel the calling to do a long retreat and be replenished (reflection following write on spirituality).

I need to address the critic in me and allow greater receptivity to change (reflection following creation of self-care plan).

—*Hannah, child/family therapist, clinical supervisor*

- *As I read this, I notice . . .*
- *I am surprised that . . .*
- *I wonder . . .*

Six Characteristics of Resilience

1. Social Support

The single most predictive factor of the capacity to manage ordinary and extraordinary levels of stress is having strong, supportive relationships. The feeling of belonging and being deeply cared for by others enhances both physical health and an overall sense of well-being (Mills and Dombeck 2005). Caring, reciprocal relationships offer opportunities to practice social skills and networking, which in turn help increase feelings of community and connection.

Paradoxically, the helping professional's work often creates a barrier to developing a strong social support system. Psychologist Irvin Yalom notes, "Too often, we therapists neglect our personal relationships. Our work becomes our life. At the end of our workday, having given so much of ourselves, we feel drained of desire for more relationship" (2002, 252).

Skovholt and Trotter-Mathison say:

> This condition [exhaustion resulting from overinvestment in work] is more intense for those who are emotionally attuned to the needs of others. There is a continual pull in which you feel torn in many directions that leaves you feeling exhausted when saying yes, guilty when saying no—it is between giving and taking, between other-care and self-care. (2011, 3)

Does this sound familiar? How do you resolve this struggle in a way that will help you not only be more resilient, but also have better overall health and life satisfaction?

Writing Prompts
- Take inventory of your social supports. Who do you rely on to listen, act, or help? Who do you call for social outings or getaway afternoons?

- Write about a time when you knew you were overloaded but couldn't or didn't ask for help. What stopped you? If you were in the same situation now, is there something you could do differently that might offer a better outcome?
- Bring to mind the area of your life that most consistently wears you down. Now bring to mind a person you encounter in this life area who you consider helpful and supportive. Write a journal letter to this person. Practice asking for help. Take note of your feelings as you write.
- Reciprocity is an important component in social support. With whom in your workplace or home life do you feel you have or could have reciprocity? Who reaches out to you for help? Write about what it might look like if you were to propose a more conscious commitment to mutual support.

2. Proactivity

According to Stephen Covey, proactivity means that "as human beings, we are responsible for our own lives. Our behavior is a function of our decisions, not our conditions. We have the initiative and responsibility to make things happen" (1989, 71).

But being proactive is more than taking initiative; it also involves responding to circumstances based on values that allow you to see yourself as having choices. Rather than reacting to an adverse situation by complaining and fault-finding, a proactive person looks at alternatives and asks, "What's another possibility?" The proactive person is neither passive nor reactive, but rather engaged in a self-confident, open way. For people whose job it is to help others, this particular resilience quality is vital. Covey says, "It's not what happens to us, but our response to what happens to us that hurts us" (1989, 73) or, in the words of Viktor Frankl (1984), "In our response lies our freedom and our growth."

Writing Prompts
- What are proactive behaviors that are already part of your routine? Make a bullet list.
- Finish this sentence ten different ways: *When I am proactive . . .*
- How's your self-talk? To check it out, set your timer for thirty minutes and proceed with your normal activities. Be mindful of your interior dialogue. Make notes whenever you hear yourself making observational comments

---

Resilience Manifesto

I am stronger every day. I cannot be stopped, I can only be slowed. With trials and struggle/adversity come experience and knowledge. I will be a patient husband, father, son, and brother. I will further my profession. I will do more than survive. I will live a life. I will really taste my food, and listen to music, and hear those I care about. I will experience all that I can. . . . I will embrace pain because through pain is growth. . . . I will have one goal above all else: Live life, experience it.

—Jacob, child/family therapist

(*This is going well!* or *You're messing up!* or *Time for a break—you need to stretch*).

- Think of someone who has transcended suffering or difficult circumstances and expressed the values of contribution, service, and self-determination. This may be a person you know, someone you knew in the past, someone in the public eye. It may even be a fictional character. Imagine that you are a newspaper reporter interviewing this person. Ask for his or her secrets to success, how she or he deals with challenges. Let yourself make up the responses, the way you think she or he might answer.

3. Gratitude

Researcher on the science of gratitude Robert Emmons found that in order to be complete, gratitude must have three parts: recognition, acknowledgment, and appreciation. More than politeness or a superficial feeling, gratitude has the ability to transform adversity into opportunity (Emmons 2007, 5–6).

Over the past two decades, research in positive psychology and in neuro-science have found that a daily gratitude practice acts as an antidote to the innate negativity bias of the brain. Resilience is a reliably measurable outcome of cultivating positive emotions such as gratitude (Graham 2013).

Gratitude opens channels. When practiced regularly, it can produce an increase in positive emotions and resilience. Sarah Ban Breathnach, author of

Simple Abundance, describes her daily practice of writing a list of five things for which she is grateful. She notes, "Real life isn't always going to be perfect or go our way, but the recurring acknowledgement of what is working in our lives can help us not only survive but surmount our difficulties" (Ban Breathnach 1995, January 14).

Gratitude is perhaps the most transformative of all the qualities of resilience, especially in times of stress or difficult circumstances. When we, as helping professionals, integrate it as a daily practice, gratitude can support the delivery of extraordinary service and care.

Writing Prompts

- Take inventory of your current gratitude practice. Where do you have consistent conscious practices? Where do you have consistent habituated practices, such as saying, "thank you" when someone opens a door, or at the end of everyday business transactions? Where do you lack gratitude practices?
- Thinking about your life as a whole, what are you grateful for? What have been the enduring qualities or conditions that have positively shaped you?
- Write a long list (strive for 100 entries) of everyday blessings—people, places, things, qualities, conditions that are real and present in your life right now.
- Write a thank-you letter to your professional self. What does she or he do exceptionally well that is deserving of gratitude?
- Graham (2013) suggests using a two-minute write remembering people who keep us functioning in the web of life, even if we've never met them personally: your garbage/recycling collector; your postal delivery person; the first responders in the emergency room, police station, or fire station; the highway construction crew.

4. Empathy

Empathy is the ability to read and appropriately respond to another's emotions. Empathy requires the capacity to connect with something in ourselves that recognizes and "knows" the feeling that another is experiencing (Brown 2013). Ekman (2011) extends this to a three-part attunement:

- you *understand* the other's feelings
- you *feel* what they are feeling
- you are *moved* to help or support them in some way

Brooks and Goldstein (2004) found that when we ask questions about another person's perspective, we increase the likelihood of understanding and empathizing with what the world is like from that person's point of view. Mills and Dombeck (2005) suggest that high-quality relationships—a key to resilience—are characterized by high levels of empathy:

> The quality of your relationships, and not the quantity of them, is what matters for you in terms of your emotional resilience. It is better to have a few high quality relationships than many lower quality ones. One of the attributes that differentiates people with higher quality relationships from people with lower quality relationships is their ability to be compassionate and empathetic.

While it is easy to have empathy for people who share our values and opinions, the challenge comes with having empathy for those with different values and mind-sets from our own. In the helping professions this situation is encountered frequently. The more we are able to see the world from someone else's perspective, which does not necessarily involve agreeing with them, the more empathic we become. If we "seek first to understand, then be understood" (Covey 1989), we will grow into empathy.

Writing Prompts
- Bring to mind a client who challenged you. Write for ten minutes about the challenges you experienced, how you responded to the challenges, and how the situation ended up. As you look back on it, were you able to grow in empathy with this client? What did this client teach you about yourself?
- What sort of personality type, belief system, or philosophical world view predictably evokes a negative reaction from you? Think about a recent encounter, then try applying Ekman's attunement process of *understanding*, *feeling*, and *helping/supporting* in your journal. Do you notice any shifts?
- The journal technique of Perspectives (Adams 1990) allows us to walk in another person's shoes. Choose someone with whom you have conflict or disagreement. Close your eyes and imagine that you are that person. Write for ten minutes in his or her first-person voice. What might be motivating or driving the conflict, from that person's perspective?
- Make a list of practical ideas of how you might extend your capacity for empathy for those with whom you do not share values or opinions.

*What Did You Learn
About Yourself Today?*

From evaluations of *Roots of Resilience* workshop with counseling professionals:

- I learned that my resilient self is my true self.
- Journaling can be and is a useful tool for my inner work.
- I have a lot of questions and doubts, but surprisingly, I also have a lot of answers if I just ask myself.
- Short, quick writing processes are effective.
- I am more resilient than I thought! I need to remind myself of this more.
- I always thought I wasn't a "journal person" but this introduction challenges that thought.

5. Realistic Optimism

Optimism is sometimes misunderstood. It is sometimes mistaken for a pop-psychology mentality in which expectations predict outcomes; optimism and "positive thinking" become substitutes for action. It is also commonly assumed that a tendency toward optimism or pessimism is an intractable personality trait, when in truth optimism is a learnable skill (Mills and Dombeck 2005).

Albert Bandura's work on self-efficacy and the role optimism plays in success found that, while one of the best predictors of success is belief in one's own success, there is an enormous difference between belief in success and belief in *easy* success. Bandura wrote about "realistic optimism," which is not only believing you will succeed, but the recognition that that you need to use effort, careful planning, persistence, and choosing the right strategies in order to achieve the success you're seeking. Success is not something that just happens; it requires recognition of how you'll deal with obstacles. This type of preparation increases your confidence in your own ability to get things done, which also contributes to your ability to bounce back when faced with adversity or difficult circumstances (Halvorson, 2012).

Writing Prompts

- What is your generalized world view? "Glass half-full" or "glass half-empty"? What are the benefits of this world view? Are there limitations or difficulties with this world view? Take an objective assessment.
- What does the phrase "realistic optimism" mean to you? How might you cultivate more of it?
- Bring to mind a time when you wanted something, and you set out to achieve it, and you were successful. Deconstruct it. How did you approach the task? What did you do when you encountered obstacles?
- Write an imaginary conversation between your Inner Pessimist and your Inner Optimist.

6. Spirituality

Christina Puchalski, Director of the George Washington Institute for Spirituality and Health, contends that "spirituality is the aspect of humanity that refers to the way individuals seek and express meaning and purpose and the way they experience their connectedness to the moment, to self, to others, to nature, and to the significant or sacred" (Puchalski 2013). There is a connection between emotional and spiritual well-being. Spirituality seeks a meaningful connection with something bigger than yourself.

Resilience researcher Brene Brown (2010) found that stories of resilience had more in common than just "bounce" factors:

> all of these stories were about spirit. . . . Spirituality is recognizing and celebrating that we are all inextricably connected to each other by a power greater than all of us, and that our connection to that power and to one another is grounded in love and compassion. Practicing spirituality brings a sense of perspective, meaning and purpose to our lives. (64)

In Brown's research, spirituality emerged as a major component of resilience.

Mindfulness and Resilience

Mindfulness—the simple practice of attention—can be the synthesizer for the six qualities of resilience. Learn to simply observe yourself, without judgment, doing the activities and behaviors that contribute both to internal stress and to internal harmony. Pay attention, and take notes on your observations.

Dr. Lynda Klau (n.d.) says, "Resilience isn't just for hard times, but it's for all times. Living resiliently represents a whole new way of being and doing." Klau emphasizes that you don't have to meditate to be mindful. When you are feeling stressed about a situation, try Klau's five-step process, and then add writing to anchor the experience into your neurological circuitry.

1. Sit in a quiet room where you won't be disturbed.
2. Close your eyes and focus your attention on your breath.
3. It's natural for your attention to become distracted. When that happens, simply return to your breath.
4. While focusing on your breath, allow your thoughts, feelings, beliefs, and body sensations to enter your awareness as you perceive the external situation.
5. Now ask yourself, *What are the facts of the situation? What are my thoughts, feelings, beliefs, and body sensations? How am I responding?*

Write your internal responses to these questions; write about the process of sitting mindfully. Reflect on what you noticed.

According to Klau, this process can bring you to your calm, reflective center. From here it is possible to deconstruct, recontextualize, and reframe your original fear-based feelings and reactions, honoring and embracing them without being their victim.

If you practice this approach not only to the stressors in your personal and professional life but to everyday living, you're positioning yourself to engage different qualities of resilience in a consistent way.

Writing Prompts
- What part does spirituality play in your life? How would you rate your level of satisfaction and fulfillment spiritually?
- Make a list of spiritual practices you currently have or would like to develop. Bring to mind an experience of profound spiritual connection or awareness. From your senses, write about the experience.
- Is there a place in nature that inspires or deepens your spiritual connection? Write about it.

Creating a Self-Care Plan to Cultivate Resilience

An aspiring comedy writer once asked Jerry Seinfeld for any "tips of the trade":

> He told me to get a big wall calendar that has a whole year on one page and hang it on a prominent wall. The next step was to get a big red magic marker. He said for each day that I do my task of writing, I get to put a big red X over that day. [Seinfeld said,] "After a few days you'll have a chain. Just keep at it and the chain will grow longer every day. You'll like seeing that chain, especially when you get a few weeks under your belt. Your only job next is to not break the chain." (Isaac 2007)

The power of consistency works just as well for cultivating resilience as it does for writing comedy material. Here is a four-step method for creating and sustaining a self-care plan to build the roots of resilience:

Step 1: Assess Your Current Level of Self-Care

In the past thirty days, what have you done to renew and recharge your—

- —**body?** List patterns for exercise, nutrition, movement meditations, healthy sleep.

- —**social/emotional connections**? List patterns for time with friends, family, colleagues; sharing activities or meals; volunteer activities; other community-based activities.
- —**mind**? List patterns for academic or intellectual pursuits such as classes, workshops, new skill development.
- —**spirit**? List patterns for activities that bring calm, awareness, harmony, such as meditation, journal writing, time in nature, attending faith community services, reading inspirational books.

What was the frequency and time allotted for each of these categories of self-care?

Step 2: Set an Activity Goal for Each Self-Care Category

Using your paper or electronic calendar, write down one activity goal for each self-care category of body, social/emotional, mind, spirit. Decide on a realistic frequency for each activity goal. Block out approximate times for each activity, including preparation and travel time. Put it on your calendar. Take your resilience appointments as seriously as you take client appointments!

Step 3: Choose an Accountability Method to Track Your Progress

Follow Jerry Seinfeld's strategy for developing consistency: Place an X or note on a calendar for visual reinforcement. If you have "blank" days, don't judge, just notice. Be honest with your progress and compassionate with your gaps. Regularly reward yourself with a small treat for consistently showing up to take care of yourself.

Step 4: Build Variety in Your Choice of Self-Care Activities

Boredom can derail self-care practices. Engage your creativity and look for new ways of renewing yourself. Ask friends and colleagues about their self-care practices. When you start to feel bored or flat, turn to your journal and ask curious questions such as *What do I want? What do I need? What would I enjoy?* Reward yourself with a fun, relaxing experience (for instance, a leisurely swim, bike ride, walk, massage) for consistently showing up to take care of yourself.

Conclusion

When we are nonjudgmentally aware of our in-the-moment experiences, both internally and externally, we can transparently observe and shift our responses. This mindful attention is the thread that connects us to resilience. We learn to embrace social support, proactivity, empathy, gratitude, realistic optimism, and spirituality as both sustainable and renewable resources.

Document this awareness through expressive writing, and we begin to see the growth of resilience over time. We can track the shift to a locus of freedom and choice rather than anxiety and exhaustion. We observe ourselves evolving into stronger, healthier, more resilient practitioners.

References

Adams, Kathleen. 1990. *Journal to the self: Twenty-two paths to personal growth.* New York: Warner Books.

———. 2013. Expression and reflection: Toward a new paradigm in expressive writing. In *Expressive writing: Foundations of practice*, edited by K. Adams. Lanham, MD: Rowman & Littlefield Education.

Ban Breathnach, Sarah. 1995. The gratitude journal. In *Simple abundance: A daybook of comfort and joy.* New York: Warner Books.

Barclay, Laurie J., and Daniel P. Skarlicki. 2009. Healing wounds of organizational injustice: Examining the benefits of expressive writing. *Journal of Applied Psychology* 94(2):511–23.

Begley, Sharon. 2013. Rewiring your emotions. *Mindful.* Accessed January 7, 2015. http://www.mindful.org/mindful-magazine/rewiring-your-emotions.

Brooks, Robert, and Sam Goldstein. 2004. *The power of resilience: Achieving balance, confidence and personal strength in your life.* New York: McGraw-Hill.

Brown, Brene. 2010. *The gifts of imperfection: Letting go of who you think you're supposed to be and embrace who you are.* Center City, MN: Hazelden.

———. 2013. The power of empathy. RSA Shorts. December 10, 2013. Accessed January 7, 2015. https://www.youtube.com/watch?v=1Evwgu369Jw.

Buckwalter, Galen. 2011. Attributes of resilience (part four). The Headington Institute blog, November 30, 2011. Accessed January 7, 2015. http://www.headington-institute.org/blog-home/163/attributes-of-resilience-part-four.

Covey, Stephen R. 1989. *The 7 habits of highly effective people: Powerful lessons in personal change.* New York: Free Press.

Dalton, Jonathan J., and David S. Glenwick. 2009. Effects of expressive writing on standardized graduate entrance exam performance and physical health functioning. *Journal of Psychology: Interdisciplinary and Applied* 143(3):279–92.

Ekman, Paul. 2011. Culture of empathy builder. Conversation with Edwin Rutsch, February 2, 2011. Accessed January 5, 2015. http://j.mp/JJDMc4.

Emmons, Robert. 2007. *Thanks! How practicing gratitude can make you happier.* Boston: Houghton Mifflin.

Frankl, Viktor. 1984. *Man's search for meaning.* New York: Touchstone.

Graham, Jennifer E., Marci Lobel, Peter Glass, and Irina Lokshina. 2008. Effects of written expression in chronic pain patients: Making meaning from pain. *Journal of Behavioral Medicine* 31(3):201–12.

Graham, Linda. 2013. *Bouncing back: Rewiring your brain for maximum resilience and well-being.* Novato, CA: New World Library.

Halvorson, Heidi Grant. 2012. Adopt a new attitude: Realistic optimism. Huffington Post Healthy Living. Accessed January 7, 2015. http://www.huffingtonpost.com/heidi-grant-halvorson-phd/optimism_b_1215644.html.

Isaac, Brad. 2007. Jerry Seinfeld's productivity secret. Lifehacker. Accessed January 4, 2015. http://lifehacker.com/281626/jerry-seinfelds-productivity-secret.

King, Laura A. 2001. The health benefits of writing about life goals. *Personality and Social Psychology Bulletin* 27(7):798–807.

King, Laura A., and Kathi N. Miner. 2000. Writing about perceived benefits of traumatic events: Implications for physical health. *Personality and Social Psychology Bulletin* 26:220–30.

Klau, Lynda. N.d. Mindfulness: The art of cultivating resilience. Accessed January 6, 2015. http://www.yourtango.com/experts/dr-lynda-klau/mindfulness-art-cultivating-resilience-expert#.VK04p3uumaE.

Mills, Harry and Mark Dombeck. 2005. Emotional resilience. Syndicated by Center Site LLC. Accessed December 29, 2014. http://www.mentalhelp.net/poc/view_doc.php?type=doc&id=5778&cn=298.

Pennebaker, James W., and Sandra K. Beall. 1986. Confronting a traumatic event: Toward an understanding of inhibition and disease. *Journal of Abnormal Psychology* 95(3): 274–81.

Pierce, Craig. 2014. (December). Personal communication.

Puchalski, Christine. 2013. What is spirituality? University of Minnesota Center for Spirituality and Healing, July 10, 2013. Accessed January 7, 2015. http://www.takingcharge.csh.umn.edu/enhance-your-wellbeing/purpose/spirituality/what-spirituality.

Skovholt, Thomas M., and Michelle Trotter-Mathison. 2011. *The resilient practitioner: Burnout prevention and self-care strategies for counselors, therapists, teachers and health professionals.* 2nd Ed. New York: Routledge Taylor.

Troncoso, Robin. 2013. How's your resilience? A self-care assessment. Albuquerque, NM: Southwest Family Guidance Center.

Yalom, Irvin. 2002. *The gift of therapy: An open letter to a new generation of therapists and their patients.* New York: HarperCollins.

10

Creating a New Story after Brain Injury

BARBARA STAHURA

What happens when brain injury turns the familiar story of a life inside out? What happens to that story when the physical and, more crucially, the cognitive abilities that form a Self are so altered they can leave people with brain injury (and their families) feeling stranded without hope in an alien world?

For many people with brain injury, the old story is gone or greatly changed. Clinging to it is useless, as well as detrimental to living a good "new normal." The healthiest thing to do is create a new, post-injury story on which to build a new life.

Traditional therapies after brain injury—speech/cognitive, physical, occupational—are essential to restoring or recovering lost abilities as much as possible and to building compensatory strategies. Yet these therapies do not offer much guidance to people in exploring changes to their former stories or in creating new stories that can foster a satisfying post-injury life. Acknowledging and accepting what has happened—essential to moving forward—is not as easily accomplished if people are stuck in their old stories and do not create new ones to build a pathway into the future.

Fortunately, brains are "organs of story, changing to match the needs of their environment" (Mehl-Madrona 2010, 13). And now that neuroscience is demonstrating the power of words to change the brain (Borchard 2013), we know it is possible to use words purposefully to change the stories of our lives in beneficial ways. As three decades of research has shown, writing adds another powerful dimension to that process. Journaling after brain injury, particularly in targeted, facilitated groups, can provide opportunities for people to change their stories using *their own words*, both to match their current realities and to discover pathways to a satisfying and productive new reality.

What Brain Injury Can Do

I tell people that each day it's like as if you went to bed and you woke up in China or New York City not knowing how you got there. It's like I don't speak the same language as everyone else anymore. Not knowing how you ended up in this strange place is how I feel all the time. (Stahura and Schuster 2009, 17)

This telling metaphor was written by Michael, who sustained a severe brain injury in a motorcycle accident. An Army veteran of the Gulf War, his former life as a telecommunications engineer was over, as was the possibility of any other career; his wife became the sole support of the family; and their life together of more than thirty years shifted into unknown territory. Many people with brain injury will identify with Michael's description of his reality.

Whatever its cause, each brain injury is as unique as the person to whom it happens; as has been said, when you've seen one brain injury, you've seen one brain injury. An injury to this mysterious, magnificent organ can affect physical function, which is difficult enough. Yet it is unique among injuries that can befall humans in that it can disrupt the most fundamental aspects of what makes us "us"—personality, memory, thought processes, emotions, motivation, self-control, the ability to learn and concentrate, self-expression, and more. Any one of these changes—let alone several—can cause confusion, stress, and worse to the injured. Furthermore, a brain injury to one person affects the entire family, which only adds to the difficulties.

Here are a few examples of the possible effects of brain injury:

- Disrupted physical functioning, ranging from walking and speaking to fine and gross motor skills to vision, taste, hearing, and smell—and more. Yet brain injury often leaves no outward signs, hence the name "the invisible injury."

- Reduced ability to create and store new memories and to access existing memories.
- Altered or diminished executive functions, which include organizing, planning, attention, problem solving, reasoning, mental flexibility, and task switching.
- Less emotional stability or more volatile emotions and reduced ability to express or read others' emotions.
- Disrupted ability to speak, read, and write, as well as to understand or comprehend written and verbal language.
- Personality changes that affect relationships, work or school, and functioning.

Common early results of the disruption caused by brain injury are denial, confusion, inability to cope with the changes, and depression. Any of these can continue for a lifetime. Yet, with proper treatment, care, and guidance, people with brain injury often are able to accept and adjust to their new reality and find healthy ways to carry on with their lives, even if they are very different from pre-injury days.

Writing and then voluntarily sharing what has been written in a friendly, respectful group of others with brain injury helps participants to feel safe and allows ideas and inspiration to spark among participants. It can be a therapeutic process that bolsters acceptance and the process of moving forward to write about

- the changes wrought by brain injury;
- the painful emotions that arrive afterward;
- finding and maintaining hope;
- positive elements that remain or may be achieved; and
- planning for the future.

"People with a brain injury often say that journaling has given them a forum for expressing their feelings about changes they have incurred," says Susan B. Schuster, MA, CCC-SLP, the speech-language pathologist ("speech therapist") who, for four years, co-facilitated my journaling groups for people with brain injury in Tucson, Arizona. "They may 'feel' changes, but writing them gives them a different release than simply talking about them."

It is as true for people with brain injury as for anyone else that, as Gillie Bolton (1999) says, "A therapeutic writing group can provide a trusted ongoing forum for the sharing of writings, hopes, fears, ideas, anticipations, tears, laughter" (127).

After Brain Injury: My Story

My husband, Ken, sustained a serious traumatic brain injury in 2003. As I was catapulted into the terrifying world of caregiving for a husband with TBI, I journaled, often pages every day, in the notebook I began carrying everywhere, a touchstone of sanity. This practice flowed mainly out of my desperate attempt to cope with a life turned upside down, potentially forever. Before long, I was diagnosed with secondary traumatic stress, and the counselor and I agreed that journaling was one of the healthiest things I could do.

At the time I was unfamiliar with the variety of journaling techniques available, and I don't know that I would have had the emotional wherewithal to use them in any case. But that notebook became my sanctuary, the safe container into which I could pour my overflowing fear and confusion, vent when necessary (which was often), keep a record of what was happening to us, and ultimately celebrate as my husband slowly recovered far more than predicted. In the process, I recovered, too.

In 2007, a comment from an acquaintance lit the spark that led me to create a journaling program for people with brain injury. I knew by then from my own journaling practice and research that writing about thoughts and feelings is beneficial to body, mind, and spirit for many disparate groups of people. Why not for people with brain injury, too?

A program of six weekly ninety-minute sessions emerged, partly inspired by a quotation from writer Deena Metzger (2002, 4): "Story. Story is my medicine." The journaling exercises in the "After Brain Injury: Telling Your Story" program follow a generalized arc of post–brain injury life. Group participants are invited to write short journal entries targeted to various aspects of their experience, and then to share those entries with the group if they so choose.

I began presenting the program at a Tucson rehabilitation hospital twice yearly until the spring of 2011, when Ken and I moved to southwestern Indiana. Now I present the program at this region's only rehabilitation hospital for people with brain injury; it has been added to the hospital's normal schedule of events and is offered once each quarter to people with any kind of brain injury, including stroke.

In 2009, the program evolved into the first journaling workbook for people with brain injury. I wrote *After Brain Injury: Telling Your Story*, with assistance from Susan B. Schuster, MA, CCC, who was instrumental in the establishment of the Tucson program. The book is in use across the country among individuals with brain injury and their family members, brain injury support groups, speech language pathologists, therapists, and others.

In order to improve my skills and further my work, I studied at the Therapeutic Writing Institute and became a certified journal facilitator in 2011. I now work primarily with people with brain injury and family caregivers of people with serious illness or injury.

Both the groups and the book offer a journaling program that encourages self-exploration and self-expression and can improve cognition and communication skills.

Journaling, Cognition, and Communication

Cognition refers to the complex collection of mental skills needed for thinking and understanding, including attention, learning, remembering, perception, comprehension, reasoning, and problem solving. Without cognition, we could neither understand the world nor function in it. Not surprisingly, people with brain injury can face long-term cognitive problems when they lose one or more of these skills.

These deficits can cause difficulty with everything from seemingly simple tasks like making a sandwich or writing a check to larger, more important areas of life, such as success at work and in school, maintaining relationships, driving or navigating the environment, and staying abreast of whatever life brings.

Cognition impacts communication, both verbal and written. Skills such as following a train of thought or a conversation (one's own or another's), being able to find and express the right words, processing information, concentrating, and creating and storing memories are all part of communication. Writing down thoughts and feelings after brain injury assists communication and cognition in many ways.

In 2007, my main intention in creating a journaling program for people with brain injury was to encourage self-expression and self-exploration after what must be one of the most bewildering, frightening experiences a human being can have. Writing in a safe, protected environment to express deep emotions and thoughts offers many benefits, including:

- release of strong feelings;
- exploration of old and new realities;
- structuring and organizing anxious feelings; and
- opportunities for reflection on what has been discovered in the writing.

In addition, writing allows people to gain perspective on their circumstances and helps them face the difficult challenges ahead, according to Dawn Westfall, MS, CCC-SLP, who co-facilitates my Indiana groups. "The journaling increases self-awareness and acceptance of their injury and their situation," she says. "Writing about their experience gives them the ability to move forward instead of constantly looking back and holding on to the past."

Expressive writing is healing and beneficial to body, mind, and spirit, as demonstrated by hundreds of clinical studies that began in the mid-1980s with James W. Pennebaker's research (Pennebaker and Beall 1986; Pennebaker 1989, 1990). When people with brain injury write about their experiences, they can explore some of the elements that now play a role in their changed lives, including the grief and loss resulting from the injury, finding and maintaining hope, dealing with challenging situations, and plans for the future. Keeping the writing specific to brain injury is important, says Westfall, "because people can relate more to it than to more generic journaling, and writing in a group that is addressing the same topics helps them feel connected."

People with brain injury are just like anyone else in their desire for friendship, understanding, respect, and support through difficult times, although they probably have more challenges in meeting this desire than other people. Like many journaling groups, the After Brain Injury groups meet regularly in a safe, friendly environment to explore what is in participants' hearts and minds and to express that in writing. Participants find community among others who truly understand, which is important because a brain injury can leave people feeling isolated and deeply misunderstood. They are encouraged to be as honest as possible in their writing and, if they choose, to share what they have written.

Allison understood she was not alone when participants in one group strongly agreed with one of her heartfelt journal entries:

> Sometimes people tell me to "snap out of it," and that makes me so MAD. Are you my brain? Do you know what I'm going through? Do you think I'm doing this on purpose? Try being in my head for a day. (Stahura and Schuster 2009, 59)

This kind of intentional writing encourages the discovery of a new life story and assists with making it a reality. It fosters new perceptions of the situation and creativity in dealing with it. Over time, this process of writing also provides a record of a life, which is especially important to someone with memory impairment. "It becomes a reference for them in their recovery, in that they can read prior writings and see changes in their feelings," says Schuster. "These changes are often viewed by them as a progression in their recovery process.

I have found that, with very few exceptions, participants in my groups do not journal, or journal with any regularity, on their own. Perhaps they forget, or they lack motivation or initiative due to the brain injury. They may prefer to write only in the group, or they simply might not have the physical or emotional energy. To encourage them to write on their own, I provide "homework" to be done in between weekly sessions, and most of the participants choose to do this. Typically the homework is to write for five to ten minutes from a prompt. The prompt may arise from the session, such as "Something I learned today . . . " or "I need help with . . . ," or I might assign different prompts to different participants, depending on topics that came up during the session. People may share their homework at the next meeting if they choose.

People often begin attending After Brain Injury groups at the invitation or request of their speech-language pathologist or other therapist, and some of them may at first be nervous or resistant. For the most part, though, their enthusiasm grows week by week, and they become more open to the writing and sharing. The stereotypical "person who journals" is a woman. Yet my groups have always included more men, possibly because more men than women sustain brain injuries. And these men have often bravely shared their emotions as much as the women and have shown as much compassion to their fellow travelers. While for some this might be a result of the changes caused by brain injury, I believe it generally is due to feeling safe and comfortable enough in the groups to open up.

"Obviously, some people have more difficulty with attention and concentration, word-finding, information processing, memory and concept formation, and the executive functioning skills-planning utilized in structured writing," says Sharron Walker, PhD, a psychotherapist who has led journaling groups for people with brain injury. "In these cases, people generally need more coaxing to attempt or focus on journal writing. However, once people began to write, they were often surprised at how much they were able to put down, how much they gained from the activity, and how much they were able to express through writing."

Further Benefits of Journaling after Brain Injury

Although journal writing is widely considered a private activity, in my groups, most of the participants share their writing most of the time. While the writing offers connection with the self, the sharing offers connection with others. Many people with brain injury feel isolated, and are in fact isolated. So when they attend these groups and discover the kind of connection that is possible with others who share life in the same boat, they often open up. All of them have a need to be understood, which encourages them to attempt to understand others—and they do this by writing and sharing the short stories of their journal entries.

"The stories people tell have a way of taking care of them," says writer Barry Lopez (1998, 60). Schuster and I saw this caretaking at work in our Tucson groups. "It has been my observation that doing at least some journaling in a group setting allows for open and honest input and feedback from others experiencing similar feelings," Schuster says. "People see that they are not alone—that others have or are going through similar adjustments. There seems to be a special connection that develops. It's one thing for someone to listen to a person with a brain injury, but it's a different connection when that someone who is listening has also had a brain injury."

Additionally, beyond my original goals of self-expression and self-exploration, in the years of facilitating these groups, the speech therapists and I have discovered numerous practical benefits that arise when people with brain injury journal in a facilitated group designed for them. Participation in the writing, sharing, and discussion:

- enhances written and verbal communication skills;
- stimulates cognitive and executive skills (following direction, organizing, planning, sequencing, attention, processing, etc.);
- promotes post-injury self-awareness (deficits and strengths);
- assists in planning for the post-injury future;
- promotes dialogue and understanding with family members and others;
- encourages self-expression after a trauma and major life disruption; and
- offers community and support.

Preparing to Facilitate Journaling for People with Brain Injury

Working with people with various cognitive deficits and often related physical difficulties means that you, as facilitator, will have to be more attentive and prepared than with other groups.

In one of my early groups, for instance, one of the participants would get lost in the maze-like building trying to find the room we were in. He was a dependable participant, so when he was late, I learned to send someone out to find him. He simply waited in the cafeteria, knowing we would come looking—a very good compensatory strategy! In another group, a man who was aphasic and hemiplegic used an augmentative communication device, pecking out words that the machine later spoke for him. This process took longer than for other participants, so he would continue writing after time was called until he had finished.

Basic Preparation and Facilitation Checklist

Planning and preparing for journaling group sessions. Keep in mind that:

- If you as the facilitator have little or no experience in understanding brain injury, having a co-facilitator who is a therapist or speech-language pathologist (SLP) can be very beneficial and help the group to run more smoothly. Additionally, an SLP can answer questions about brain injury and its effects that you may not be able to answer. (To educate yourself, see Resources at the end of this chapter.)
- Brain injury can cause physical and mental fatigue, so make sessions no longer than ninety minutes (or possibly less, depending on the group).
- Consider calling or e-mailing participants before each session to remind them to attend.
- Transportation may be a problem for some participants, so decide if you want to help them find transportation to the sessions. A participant's SLP or therapist can be a valuable resource here.
- Have extra pens and inexpensive journals available. It is also a good idea to have tissues on hand.

During sessions, remember that some participants may:

- Be eager to write but have difficulty collecting their thoughts or converting thoughts into writing.
- Be easily distracted from their writing or have a short attention span.
- Forget the writing topic and need a gentle reminder.
- Be unable to write by hand due to motor difficulties or other situations; some may be able to use a laptop, tablet, or augmentative communication device for journaling.
- Have large disparities in the amount they can write at any one time, which does not necessarily reflect their enthusiasm or determination.

Pay attention to participants and be prepared to:

- Repeat or rephrase instructions so everyone understands.
- Scribe without changes or judgment for participants who cannot write or use a keyboard but can speak their journal entries, or have a helper ready to do this.
- Read aloud the journal entries of those participants who want to share their writing but cannot speak, or have a helper ready to do this.
- Gently encourage those who are reluctant to write or voluntarily share.
- Remind participants that whatever they write is right for that moment and that no judgment or criticism of their writing will be allowed, although positive comments are encouraged.
- Deviate from the planned activity if the situation warrants.

Cautions

- Particularly in a health facility, privacy concerns under HIPAA (Health Insurance Portability and Accountability Act) in the United States require strict confidentiality of all health information of inpatients, outpatients, and former patients. So emphasize the confidential nature of the journaling groups, and repeat as necessary.
- Writing can elicit strong emotions in any journaling group. Yet some people with brain injury may have difficulty controlling their emotions: They may cry or laugh without apparent reason, make inappropriate statements, or have angry outbursts. Others may be unable to express their own emotions or read others' emotions.

Some Sample Journal Exercises and Prompts

It has been my experience that people who repeatedly attend the six-week groups continue to find new perspectives from which to write with the same prompts. Also, there are far too many exercises to be covered in six ninety-minute sessions, so different ones can be chosen each time (or more sessions can be added). The exercises work as well for people who have more recently sustained a brain injury as for those who are years out. If they attend the groups over time, as many have done, they will be able to see their perspectives and insights change.

After Brain Injury: Telling Your Story offers scores of prompts and various journaling techniques specifically aimed at people with brain injury. The six chapters (with a seventh containing miscellaneous prompts) cover a generalized arc of life after brain injury, beginning with the cause itself. While not every participant will have followed this arc, the exercises are wide-ranging enough to provide participants with a rich variety to choose from.

Invite participants to write to the prompts in each chosen exercise. Yet, it is important to remind them that they need not write to the prompt if it makes them too uncomfortable or if they have something on their minds they would rather write about. Anyone can choose to "free write" as an option at any time.

Here are a few representative prompts:

- This is how it feels to be me today . . .
- A brain injury is like . . .
- Write a dialogue with your brain or something or someone else.
- To regain my balance, I need . . .
- I want to become more resilient, and so I will . . .
- Once upon a time there was a person named (your name) who had a brain injury and now . . . (written in third person)
- Write a letter that will not be sent, with examples of prompts to start.
- If I could tell the story of what most angers me about my brain injury, I would say . . .
- I am the only one who can say what my life means, and I say it means . . .
- Being back home . . .
- One of my best stories about myself is . . .
- One thing that no one can take away from me is . . .

The prompts offer many opportunities to look at post-injury life in new ways. Inviting someone with brain injury to write both sides of a dialogue with someone who doesn't understand the changes caused by the injury is an opportunity to plan a conversation that could remedy relationship difficulties or open the door to more self-understanding. One woman was unrelentingly negative about her life after several strokes; yet when for homework I asked her to write a simple list of ten positive things in her life, no matter how small they seemed, she was happily surprised, and her outlook began to improve. And Lesley, who was about twenty years out from her injury, wrote this about "one of the best stories about myself":

> A stampede of horses changed the story of my life by causing me to focus on what is right here, right now. The brain injury I experienced was severe enough to keep me hospitalized for three and a half months then under nursing care at home for another month. . . . I appreciate more now and that lesson doesn't go away. I cherish what I have and focus on the benefits of the friends and family around me. My brain injury was a life affirming experience for me. (Stahura and Schuster 2009, 89)

Like Lesley, some people have found their brain injury to be a life affirming experience. Others consider their brain injury to be the worst thing that ever happened to them. Yet wherever on that spectrum people find themselves, they benefit from being able to express their true feelings about their experiences. One effective way to do that is to participate in a safe, facilitated journaling group designed for them. There, they have the opportunity to discover more about themselves and their changed lives, perhaps change their perspective in a more positive direction, and enjoy the kind of gentle yet powerful self-exploration that few other methods provide.

References

Bolton, Gillie. 1999. *The therapeutic potential of creative writing: Writing myself.* London: Jessica Kingsley.

Borchard, Therese J. 2013. "Words can change your brain." *World of Psychology.* Accessed June 3, 2014. http://psychcentral.com/blog/archives/2013/11/30/words-can-change-your-brain/.

Brain Injury Association of America. N.d. What is the difference between an acquired brain injury and a traumatic brain injury? Accessed January 29, 2014. http://www.biausa.org/FAQRetrieve.aspx?ID=43913.

———. March 18, 2013. New data shows 3.5 million people sustain a TBI each year. Accessed January 29, 2014. http://www.biausa.org/announcements/new-data-shows-3-5-million-people-sustain-a-tbi-each-year.

Centers for Disease Control and Prevention. 2014. What are the leading causes of TBI? Accessed January 29, 2014. http://www.cdc.gov/TraumaticBrainInjury/get_the_facts.html.

———. March 6, 2014. "Traumatic brain injury." Accessed May 30, 2014. http://www.cdc.gov/traumaticbraininjury/.

Defense and Veterans Brain Injury Center. N.d. TBI and the military. Accessed July 16, 2014. http://dvbic.dcoe.mil/tbi-military.

Lopez, Barry. 1998. *Crow and weasel.* New York: Farrar, Straus and Giroux.

Mehl-Madrona, Lewis. 2010. *Healing the mind through the power of story: The promise of narrative psychiatry.* Rochester, VT: Bear and Company.

Metzger, Deena. 2002. *Entering the ghost river.* Topanga, CA: Hand to Hand.

Pennebaker, James W. 1989. Confession, inhibition, and disease. *Advances in Experimental Social Psychology* 22:211–44.

———. 1990. *Opening up: The healing power of expressing emotions.* New York: Guilford.

Pennebaker, James W., and Sandra Beall. 1986. Confronting a traumatic event: Toward an understanding of inhibition and disease. *Journal of Abnormal Psychology* 95:274–81.

Stahura, Barbara, and Susan B. Schuster. 2009. *After brain injury: Telling your story.* Wake Forest, NC: Lash & Associates Publishing/Training.

Tanielian, Terri, and Lisa H. Jaycox, eds. 2008. *The invisible wounds of war: Psychological and cognitive injuries, their consequences, and services to assist recovery.* Santa Monica, CA: RAND. Accessed November 2, 2014. http://www.rand.org/content/dam/rand/pubs/monographs/2008/RAND_MG720.pdf.

Texas Health and Human Services Commission. N.d. "Office of Acquired Brain Injury." Accessed January 29, 2014. http://www.hhsc.state.tx.us/hhsc_projects/abj/.

Additional Resources

This section contains excellent resources for first-person and reader-friendly clinical information about brain injury.

Memoirs by People with Brain Injury or about Their Family Members

Biagioni, Janelle Breese. 2004. *A change of mind: One family's journey through brain injury.* Wake Forest, NC: Lash & Associates Publishing/Training.

Coskie, Dixie Fremont-Smith. 2010. *Unthinkable: A mother's terror, tragedy, and triumph through a child's traumatic brain injury.* Deadwood, OR: Wyatt-MacKenzie.

Crimmins, Cathy. 2000. *Where is the mango princess? A journey back from brain injury.* New York: Random House.

Cromer, Janet. 2010. *Professor Cromer learns to read: A couple's new life after brain injury.* Bloomington, IN: AuthorHouse.

Grant, David. 2012. *Metamorphosis: Surviving brain injury.* CreateSpace.

Long, P. J. 2005. *Gifts from the broken jar: Rediscovering hope, beauty, and joy.* Culver City, CA: EquiLibrium Press.

Osborn, Claudia L. 1998. *Over my head: A doctor's own story of head injury from the inside looking out.* Kansas City, MO: Andrews McNeel.

Rawlins, Rosemary. 2011. *Learning by accident.* Denver, CO: Outskirts Press.

Taylor, Jill Bolte. 2009. *My stroke of insight: A brain scientist's personal journey.* New York: Viking Penguin.

Reader-Friendly Information about Brain Injury

Byler, John C. 2012. *You look great! Strategies for living inside a brain injury.* CreateSpace.

Doidge, Norman. 2007. *The brain that changes itself: Stories of personal triumph from the frontiers of brain science.* New York: Viking Penguin.

Senelick, Richard, and Karla Dougherty. 2001. *Living with brain injury: A guide for families.* 2nd ed. Birmingham, AL: HealthSouth Press.

Stoler, Diane Roberts, and Barbara Albers Hill. 2013. *Coping with concussion and mild traumatic brain injury: A guide to living with the challenges associated with post concussion syndrome and brain trauma*. New York: Avery Trade.

Swierchinsky, Dennis P. 2002. *Normal again: Redefining life after brain injury*. Lincoln, NE: Writer's Showcase.

Online Resources

Brain Injury Association of America—www.biausa.org

BrainLine—www.brainline.org

Centers for Disease Control and Prevention—www.cdc.gov/traumaticbraininjury

Defense and Veterans Brain Injury Center—http://www.dvbic.org

Basic Facts about Brain Injury

Traumatic brain injury is "caused by a bump, blow or jolt to the head or a penetrating head injury that disrupts the normal function of the brain. Not all blows or jolts to the head result in a TBI. The severity of a TBI may range from 'mild,' i.e., a brief change in mental status or consciousness to 'severe,' i.e., an extended period of unconsciousness or amnesia after the injury" (Centers for Disease Control and Prevention 2014). Note that a "mild" TBI refers to the severity of the physical trauma that caused the injury, not its potential consequences, which can be life-altering.

TBIs are a subset of acquired brain injury, which is an injury to the brain that occurs after birth. It is not hereditary, congenital, degenerative, or induced by birth trauma (Brain Injury Association of America n.d.). These brain injuries result from stroke, oxygen deprivation, infection, substance abuse, some toxic exposures, and metabolic disorders such as diabetic coma (Texas Health and Human Services Commission n.d.).

Regardless of the cause, brain injuries can produce similar results and can be devastating to a person's life and well-being. Proper diagnosis and treatment can still be a hit-or-miss proposition, particularly with milder injuries, due to inadequate training of medical personnel, low sophistication of imaging techniques, and the fact that many brain injuries show no outward signs, not to mention the mysterious nature of the brain, which we have only just begun to decipher.

The Centers for Disease Control and Prevention provides telling statistics about traumatic brain injury in the United States:

- At least 3.5 million TBIs occur every year (Brain Injury Association of America 2013).
- TBI is a contributing factor to 30.5 percent of all injury-related deaths.
- About 75 percent of TBIs that occur are concussions or other forms of mild TBI (which, if not properly diagnosed and treated, can have drastic results).
- The most likely to sustain a TBI are children age four and under, adolescents age fifteen to nineteen, and adults age sixty-five and older.
- Adults seventy-five and older have the highest rates of TBI-related hospitalization and death.
- In every age group, TBI rates are higher for males than females.
- In 2000, the direct medical costs and indirect costs such as lost productivity due to TBI totaled an estimated $76.5 billion.

The leading causes of TBI are falls (35.2 percent), motor vehicle and traffic incidents (17.3 percent), struck by/against events (16.5 percent), and assaults (10 percent). In the military, service members face a higher risk of sustaining a TBI than do their civilian peers. One 2008 report estimates that 320,000 troops experienced at least one, and often more, probable TBI during deployment in Iraq and Afghanistan (Tanielian and Jaycox 2008).

11

After the Deep Dive

Reflections on Writing beyond Cancer

JEAN ROWE

Cancer is a traumatic experience.[1] As an oncology social worker who has borne witness to the cancer journey since 2005, I know this to be true. The trauma is paradoxical. There is the "deep dive" of treatment, and then there is this moment at the end of the "deep dive," a year to eighteen months after you have been diagnosed when suddenly you're not going to the doctor all the time. You don't have to come back for three months for scans. You are cut loose.

This is a good thing, but it also elicits what we might consider a counter intuitive reaction from cancer survivors. Survivors routinely report how they are fearful about not seeing the doctor and the doctor not having eyes and ears on them. During the "deep dive," doctors, nurses, and others are keeping in touch with them and looking after them constantly. Not going back for three months brings up anxiety such as *what if the cancer's still lurking somewhere and no one knows about it?*

As I was working toward my certification as a journal therapist and working as an oncology social worker at the Winship Cancer Institute of Emory University in Atlanta, I started a journal writing group called *Just Write*. My extraordinarily small marketing campaign consisted of a sales pitch stating that writing is good for you. I backed it up with research that said so (Stanton and Danoff-Burg 2002).

What better advertisement than responses shared by both practitioners and clients about the benefits of writing? Descriptions of its benefits in the research include participants stating journal writing is "extremely helpful," "essential," and "effective in facilitating change." Practitioners describe clients "making faster progress," being "less anxious," and "better able to organize and structure their experiences" (Adams 1999).

For four years of the *Just Write* groups, I encountered survivors who were past that "deep dive" of treatment. That did not mean that people were finished with treatment altogether, but they were either going to be watched for a while or they were going to be taking some sort of maintenance therapy (Cancer.Net 2013) that did not require them being in the oncologist's office as often.

Just Write Launches

My first *Just Write* group was composed of five people: three young women ranging from age thirty to forty-two, all diagnosed with breast cancer, two with early stage, one with stage IV. There were also two gentlemen in their late fifties to early sixties, both with gastrointestinal cancers.

They were an unlikely gathering of people. Cancer will do that.

During the first couple of meetings, the group members had to find their way of how to be themselves, one with each other. Cindy, at age thirty the youngest in the group, came in after a year to a year and a half of treatment for early stage breast cancer. She was taking Tamoxifen[2] and was participating in a clinical trial. She was deeply angry about her life being turned upside down by cancer and by experiencing things a thirty-year-old woman should not be experiencing, like going through early menopause. She loved to let the "F bombs" fly, and she and Jason, who was a deeply devout person of faith, had to navigate being in the same room and being authentic. Cindy told Jason that she liked to express all kinds of wickedly inappropriate things and that he was going to have to be okay with that. Jason was giving and loving in his response and told her that she needed to be however she wanted and needed to be and that they would be just fine. They were.

Jason was focused on the introspective, personal writing about what happened to him and continually expressed a desire to give back.

Danny came to the group, I think, more at the urging of his wife and may have been somewhat skeptical about being in this group. He, however, thoroughly immersed himself and became one of the group's biggest advocates. Danny wrote what I would describe as cowboy poetry with titles like *Radiation Barbecue.* He was an avid gardener and shared the bounty at our meetings, showering us with all manner of tomatoes and peppers. He called me "Teach."

Julie was metastatic from the day she was diagnosed as a breast cancer survivor. This means breast cancer leaves the breast, and it typically goes to one of several places: the brain, the liver, the lung, or the bone. Cancer spread to her sternum, and Julie was on treatment without a break for nearly three and a half years. She took part in all of the groups that I started and managed while at Winship. In addition to *Just Write*, she joined a breast cancer support group specifically for young women and a breast cancer support group for metastatic breast cancer for women of all ages. I saw her practically on a daily basis.

Susan was a quiet member of our group but very much wanted a seat at the table. She did do the writing and sometimes she did share, but mainly she just wanted to be there.

This raises an important point about groups in general. There are some people who want to share a lot and will be quite talkative, and then there are some people who are not (Frey and Frey 2004). The reasons vary, but in journal groups, quiet participants may percolate at a slower pace, need quiet and time to reflect not just in their journals but in their minds, before they even get it into their journals. It's important to allow for that space and to check in with people not just at the end of that particular group meeting but again at subsequent meetings. They often have more to say.

The role of facilitator is vital in nurturing the quiet participant's sharing in his or her way, in his or her time. Equally important is the gentle reminder to the prolific, sharing participant to allow space and time for all to share. Nurturing curiosity in all participants, encouraging them to approach what surfaces with love and openness as well as guiding understanding and insight are all possible roles for the facilitator. Providing structure, containment, and acceptance are ongoing facilitator responsibilities (Leiberman and Golant 2002).

One of the things that I have learned about working with cancer survivors is that it becomes important to keep things in the present moment. We started simply, metaphorically warming our hands by the fire to get used to this idea of journaling, particularly in a group. Sentence Stems from the book *Journal to the Self* (Adams 1990) are a good place to get going. Instead of just one sentence stem, I offered them a list to complete. Like this:

1. What gets me out of the bed each morning is . . .
2. By my next birthday, I would like to have . . .
3. One of the most interesting people I know is . . .

Individuals would then pick one of these completed sentence stems and write a reflection about it ("As I read this, I notice . . ." or "I am surprised by . . ." or "I am aware of . . .") (Adams 2013) and maybe even set a goal.

Normal as I Know It

Another exercise we tried was writing about *Normal as I Know It*. The results allowed a look into each of their lives: How did their day begin? Who shared that space with them? What is Normal today? "Normal" changes, but that does not necessarily have to be scary. What can surface is the reminder that not everything is about cancer. Cancer does not define them or their lives. It might be the reason it got them to the group, but cancer is not a group member.

Word Jar

I cut up scraps of paper and put either a word or a phrase on each one, crumpled them up, placed them in a jar that I put on the table at each meeting. Sometimes, a member picked one piece of paper if we had time, if the group agreed that was what they wanted to do. There were no rules except one: if even just one person did not like what was drawn, it was tossed in the trash, and they would choose again.

One example might be the word *Family*. *Just Write* was an ongoing group, so holidays came and went; writing about and experiencing family, particularly with cancer, became a kind of coping mechanism. The members would return after Thanksgiving, swap recipes, and talk about That Thing That Got Said That They Couldn't Believe. Then, we'd write about it. After being with family, it is revealing for participants to see what influences their identities and belief systems. They may consider what role they play in their families, what values they were raised to believe.

Who Am I Now?

Cancer survivors experience existential concerns as a result of the commonly held notion that cancer leads to death (Henoch and Danielson 2009). Their identities are shaken. Their belief systems are challenged. They express difficulty getting past cancer. When questions come up like "who am I now?" and "what do I want to do with my life now?" I encourage the opportunity in those questions. I turned those questions around into writing prompts that had more to do with "what do you want to do?" and "I am." This nurtured feelings of being in control after a time of chaos. Writing answers to those questions in the present moment may have different answers in a month. When cancer is in the mix, my point is this: we were not writing "in five years I want to be . . ."

One of the most powerful journal prompts that we did in our group is the *List of 100* (Adams 1990). The intention is to respond to a prompt like "100 things I want to do" in one sitting, in a fast and furious list. You keep the pen moving; you do not stop until that list is finished, you repeat as often as you like; then you go back at the end of it and you categorize. How many times on a single list did "I want to be a breast cancer advocate" appear? How about, "I want to make love without fear or pain?" You tally the different percentages. You then see where, consciously or not, your thoughts, patterns, and priorities are showing up.

Danny

Just Write became a bridge for survivors who finished the "deep dive" to have the chance to obtain sure footing. While in the group, Danny enjoyed unexpected and profound connections with his adult children. Although formerly not particularly close, journal writing and poetry invited the opportunity to nurture connectedness with his family. While Danny's son was serving in Afghanistan, they experienced a whole new level in their relationship while keeping in touch about what they were each writing.

It became clear in his writing that he and his wife were going to spend as much time as they could in the Florida Keys, a place they loved. The focus was not about how much time Danny had. He was not living his life as if his last days were before him, but he had come face to face with his mortality. He focused on the things he loved best.

One exercise the group was encouraged to play with involved hanging a wind chime in an unlikely spot, a public place, and then hiding to observe public reactions to it. This idea is from an initiative called *Learning to Love You More* (July and Fletcher 2002). Danny ended up hanging a wind chime in a nearby public shower next to the beach in the Florida Keys. He then shared in the group, having fun writing about people noticing or not. He also wrote about a bird that became interested in the wind chime. His enthusiasm was palpable.

Cindy

Cindy did not want to continue with the job she had. She was writing for a daytime television show, worked from home and got paid well, but, for her, it lacked meaning. Something shifted inside of her after she became a breast cancer survivor.

Because my work has largely been with young women surviving breast cancer, they are my best examples. They are at a time in their life when, particularly in their late twenties to early thirties, they may be thinking about starting a family. They may be considering who they want their mate to be, what qualities that person needs to have. They may be considering career changes or career development. They may be thinking about going back to school. These are all normal life stage development concerns for young women at that age (Adams et al. 2011). They are not expecting cancer to be part of their lives because it is still largely viewed as an "old person's disease," and they are not expecting to be going through early menopause. Many young women are told that they will be put into menopause because of chemotherapy, and they understand that that means they will have hot flashes and might experience vaginal dryness. Beyond that, they do not know what it means. They are often bewildered by the loss of their sexual identity (Anllo 2000).

Cindy became an avid advocate for the reality that young women can and do get breast cancer. She passionately advocated for awareness, for research, and, ultimately, for acceptance that this group is larger than we think it is, even though, statistically, the numbers appear small. It became quite clear in her *List of 100 Things I Want to Do* that Cindy wanted to leave being a writer for daytime television in order to become an involved breast cancer advocate. Cindy took action toward something in which she truly believed and became a volunteer, then a staff member, for the Young Survival Coalition (YSC). She became passionately involved as an advocate both locally and nationally for young women affected by breast cancer.

The Scar

Another prompt from the *Learning to Love You More* website is to photograph a scar and tell its story. It is important to note that what scar to photograph is not part of the direction. It is important to note that the scar did not have to be on the writer's body. I gave the prompt as homework, and when group members returned two weeks later, they were angry. The members who were in the room that day were three young breast cancer survivors and one gastrointestinal cancer survivor, all women. The breast cancer survivors were outraged that I would suggest writing about a scar. I told them that I could take their anger and to share freely. I gently pointed out that the prompt was not specific to the type of scar. One person commented, "Yeah, well, if I'd chosen to write about a scar on my chin when I fell off my bike as a kid, that would be cheating." That brought forth a rich discussion about the rules she was placing on herself. By the end of the meeting, the mood shifted from anger to possibility. Maybe they would write about the scar after all.

Because *Just Write* was a group that met over several years, group membership changed over time. Although some members sadly passed away, others went on with their lives. The fact that people move on indicates that the group has done its job. The members have crossed the bridge mentioned earlier, with the help of the other group members and the facilitator's leadership and shepherding (Hepworth, Rooney, and Larsen 2002)

Getting Your Groove Back

As my work continued with young women and breast cancer, the themes around intimacy and sex continued to come up over and over again, particularly after treatment was finished (Anllo 2000; Karabulut and Erci 2009). Because of this common thread, I included as part of my journaling work writing a curriculum entitled *Getting Your Groove Back: Re-Establishing Intimacy after Cancer* for young women surviving breast cancer.

The gathering of young women who came together in one group were all young mothers, all in their thirties with small children. They came in wanting me to say, "Here, take this pill and you will be fine," and they were visibly frustrated when I didn't have an easy answer for them. They were downright flabbergasted when I told them the first relationship where they needed to reestablish intimacy was with themselves.

Kathy was well past that "deep dive," her hair fully grown back, taking Tamoxifen. She was in early menopause; she reported vaginal dryness and that her libido was almost nonexistent. The rest of the participants nodded in agreement about her libido comment and agreed that sex was painful, even with products designed to help. One woman said, "It feels like 1,000 tiny knives down there." Kathy commented that she didn't care if she ever had sex again. I asked if that's what she really wanted for her marriage and for herself as a young woman. She responded with white-hot anger. "No, it's *not* what I want, but *you* tell me, you tell *me* how to change this." I said, "You have to be willing to do something differently."[3]

We kicked off the group with this journal prompt: *What I make up about my body*. Some of the reflections were:

- I'm broken down there.
- Every ache and pain is cancer.
- If I'd never had cancer, my husband would treat me as a sexual being rather than a fragile creature.

Because of the group setting, I witnessed a sense of validation being shared, of the members realizing that they truly were not alone in their thoughts, that what they were experiencing is common. What began for them in isolation moved to a shared experience in a safe environment where they could freely discuss their frustration.

Using a journal prompt known as the Cluster (Adams 1990), I drew a big circle in the middle of a flip chart and wrote inside, *No-Guilt Date Night for One (a/k/a Sacred Alone Time)*. I then asked for their ideas and brainstorms, which I spun off into satellite circles, connected to the main idea with lines or arrows. The outshoots included bubble baths, wine, books, dog cuddles, and a "good old-fashioned bitch session." The Cluster was done as a group exercise, and when it was complete, the encouragement from me was for them to treat themselves to at least one of these things before we gathered again. They did.

One of the most powerful journal exercises we did in the Groove group is an original exercise I crafted called the *Fishbowl* exercise. I placed one fishbowl on the table and had lots of little scraps of paper and Sharpie pens. Participants write down all the words that come to mind when they think of the word *love* even if they write the same word over and over again, or even if there's no repetition. They write whatever words come up when they think what about what love means to them and they put all the scraps of paper in that fishbowl.

The first fishbowl is removed and another empty one takes its place. I told them that this fishbowl represents sex: write down all the words that come to mind about sex; even if you have some repetition. The third fishbowl was intimacy. With the group's permission, one of the members read aloud the words placed in the fishbowl for *love* while another participant made a chart with three columns for each of these words and placed hash marks beside any of the things that were repetitive in the bowl. For example, if the word *touch* was repeated three times under the heading of love, you would see the word *touch* with three hash marks out to the side. This was repeated for both the *sex* and *intimacy* fishbowls. We then made note of where words crossed categories.

The profound result revealed how mixed up *intimacy* and *love* are with *sex* and how none of these young women had any idea how wrapped up their belief systems were around the idea that love, sex, and intimacy were not separate, one from the other. It appeared that this notion had not occurred to them. They realized they were making assumptions.

In considering these three to be separate, one from the other, it raised hope and notions of opportunity. For Kathy, I asked when she and her husband were able to be alone. It did not have to involve plans. It did not have to involve spending money. It just needed to be time together. She argued with me that they did not have any time; they both worked full time; they had a toddler; they were tired and doing the best they can; no, no they just did not have any time.

I suggested that they could perhaps intentionally build time to spend together. Kathy looked dubious and said she would think about that. At subsequent meetings, Kathy told us that she and her husband were getting up thirty minutes earlier than they normally would to take a shower together, and she was really happy about this. She was *happy* that she was able to be in front of him naked after having breast surgery and that they could be close together without it being about sexual intercourse.

Love, sex, and *intimacy* as three independent ideas gave Kathy permission to try something different.

The Groove group wrote about feeling hopeful for themselves based on Kathy's courageous steps. They got into rich conversations about being clear about how they feel nourished and nurtured in their primary relationships.

One journal prompt is *How do you feel cared for (nourished, nurtured) by your spouse?* or *How does your spouse feel cared for (nourished, nurtured) by you?* Daisy, a participant, emphatically argued, "Well, I know the only way my husband feels nourished and connected with me is through sex." I asked, "How do you know that's true?" Daisy continued arguing, maintaining her point. I firmly and gently stood my ground. "Okay," I said, "but I suggest that you ask him if that's true. If it *is* true then fine, but if it's *not* true you might learn something."

She came back the next week and told us that he said he did feel nourished in other ways besides sex that had more to do with her and spending time together. Daisy's belief system was challenged. Although initially she felt a little bit of surprise and perhaps confusion, she now had new information to guide her, without the need for assumptions. This started with a journal prompt in the form of a question.

Daisy also loved to talk about how she used to be fun, used to "put out" and used to be skinny. These comments and others like it offered a segue to the journal prompt known as Dialogue (Progoff 1992). The dialogue for the Groove group is one with their bodies. The dialogue format is written in a play or script format, with two voices (in this case, one was the body's "voice") asking and answering in turn. I again challenged Daisy: "If I'm your body now, I wonder if I'm ever going to be able to be accepted by you again, the way I am now."

It gave her and everyone else in the room pause for thought. They were all young women and still very much concerned with the way they look and their sexuality. Many of them believed that they would have succeeded in life somehow if they were the way that they used to be (Siegel and Gorey 1999).

In dialoguing with the body for five to seven minutes, followed with three or four minutes of personal feedback, Daisy came away with a reflection that she needed to do "a lot less bitching and a lot more cherishing." That was a beautiful first step in claiming herself as she is now. It was a small and powerful shift in thinking. All of the members wanted their old lives back. I reminded them that whoever they were prior to cancer was still with them, that had not changed, but cancer had also come into their lives and was now part of their life story, like it or not. They could either live in the past, which they could not change, or they could choose to live in the present and fully claim their lives now.

Living in the present, giving themselves permission to try something new, opportunity. These became the undercurrent and foundations in the Groove group for inviting real change.

By the end of the six weeks, one of the swan song journal prompts was a three-part write: (a) a list of *Ten of My Favorite Things*, (b) a list of *Ten Acts of Courage* and (c) a *Self-Care Plan*. Once the first two lists are complete, we look at where any crossover exists. One example from the favorite things list was one person who was going to travel to Japan. She loved to travel, and when she looked at her courageous act list, she had listed learning a different language. Another young woman listed mountains on her favorite list and realized her courageous act list included a move to Colorado.

To craft an action plan for self-care, the participants chose three things from their plans that they really wanted to focus on. They then would pick the one thing they wanted to work toward first, then identify one step toward making that happen.

Parting reflections included these statements:

- I wouldn't have been able to make this list [of self-care action steps] at the beginning of this group. I can make it now.
- It's okay to be where I am.
- I'm going to be more active; this is my second chance.
- My feelings are normal.

Be Prepared, Then Throw Away the Lesson Plan

Sometimes participants will come to the group and share that they either simply did not do the journal prompts suggested or that they created one on their own. I learned that my role as facilitator was to be flexible and not to try to force anyone to do any particular prompt. I wanted the members to write about what was organically surfacing for them. As a new facilitator, I internally panicked that I would not know what to do. In supervision, I was always given the permission to suggest prompts on the spot and/or get the group to suggest. Nothing bad happened! Getting their feedback and watching them encourage one another often trumped, in the best way, prepared prompts.

Staying open allows the facilitator to create in the moment and receive the creativity of the group members.

Areas for Further Development

One "pink elephant" in the room is grief. While members are motivated to "get their lives back," grief is often swept under the carpet, ignored, and denied. However, the thing about grief is that it is patient. It will show up later when the timing feels odd.

One participant said, "If you make me go there, it will be bad." I remarked that I cannot make anyone do anything, but I reminded her that the grief was not going to go away. Another participant said, "It feels like I'm poking the dragon." One of her fellow participants replied, "You signed up for this."

I have no map for grief. I do have a journaling curriculum for grief and loss in all its myriad forms and experiences (loss of a loved one, physical loss, loss of hopes and dreams, existential loss); a version specific to cancer survivors is under development.

Another limitation is that the research has merely scratched the surface of what young women affected by breast cancer experience. Existing studies often ask the same questions regarding depression, anxiety, and how quality of life is impacted. They identify how young women's life stage development is thwarted. The choice whether or not to have children, for example, shifts to possibly not being able to have children at all. A young woman's career may be placed on hold or come to an end because of treatment, stage of breast cancer, and long-term side effects.

These studies are valid, of course, but they need to go further. Interventions need to be implemented. Studies need not continue to ask questions like "Have you experienced depression?" What young woman with breast cancer wouldn't experience depression? We need to become more curious about the actual experience of the patient. We need to ask questions like, "If you became depressed, were you offered the opportunity to talk to a counselor? Were you offered medication? Were you offered group support? If yes, and you took action, what helped, and how? If you didn't take action, why not?"[4]

Looking for preexisting conditions influences research results. Knowing whether someone has been treated prior to a cancer diagnosis for depression and anxiety impacts research findings.

Lastly, no one is doing longitudinal research on how journal writing impacts the cancer journey, or the long-range impact of a journal group facilitated by a professional trained in best-practice methods. It is time for a long-term study in which survivors are followed with journal prompts at different points in time (e.g., newly diagnosed, post treatment, long-term survivorship, end of life) and offered writing groups to support each stage.

References

Adams, E., L. McCann, J. Armes, A. Richardson, D. Stark, E. Watson, and G. Hubbard. 2011. The experiences, needs and concerns of younger women with breast cancer: A meta-ethnography. *Psycho-Oncology* 20:51–861.

Adams, K. 1990. *Journal to the self: Twenty-two paths to personal growth.* New York: Warner Books.

———. 1999. Writing as therapy. *Counseling and Human Development* 31:1–16.

———. 2013. Expression and reflection: Toward a new paradigm in expressive writing. In *Expressive writing: Foundations of practice,* edited by K. Adams. Lanham, MD: R&L Education.

Anllo, L. M. 2000. Sexual life after breast cancer. *Journal of Sex and Marital Therapy* 26:241–48.

Cancer.Net. 2013. Maintenance chemotherapy. Reviewed March 2013. Accessed February 22, 2015. http://www.cancer.net/navigating-cancer-care/how-cancer-treated/chemotherapy/maintenance-chemotherapy.

Cooper, M. G., and J. G. Lesser. 2002. *Clinical social work practice: An integrated approach.* Needham Heights, MA: Allyn & Bacon.

Frey, L. R., and S. Frey. 2004. The symbolic-interpretive perspective on group dynamics. *Small Group Research* 35:277–306.

Hampton, M. R., and I. Frombach. 2000. Women's experience of traumatic stress in cancer treatment. *Health Care for Women International* 21:67–76.

Henoch, I., and E. Danielson. 2009. Existential concerns among patients with cancer and interventions to meet them: An integrative literature review. *Psycho-Oncology* 18:225–36.

Hepworth, D., R. Rooney, and J. Larsen. 2002. *Direct social work practice: Theory and skills.* Pacific Grove, CA: Brooks/Cole.

July, M., and H. Fletcher. 2002. Learning to love you more. Accessed July 24, 2014. http://www.learningtoloveyoumore.com/.

Karabulut, N., and B. Erci. 2009. Sexual desire and satisfaction in sexual life affecting factors in breast cancer survivors after mastectomy. *Journal of Psychosocial Oncology* 27:332–43.

Lieberman, M. A., and M. Golant. 2002. Leader behaviors perceived by cancer patients in professionally directed support groups and outcomes. *Group Dynamics: Theory, Research and Practice* 6:267–76.

Mehnert, A., and U. Koch. 2007. Prevalence of acute and post-traumatic stress disorder and comorbid mental disorders in breast cancer patients during primary cancer care: A prospective study. *Psycho-Oncology* 16:181–88.

National Cancer Institute. 2012. NCI dictionary of cancer terms. Accessed February 22, 2015. http://www.cancer.gov/dictionary?cdrid=45576.

Progoff, I. 1992. *At a journal workshop.* Los Angeles: J. P. Tarcher.

Rowe, J., and M. Esser. 2013. It's about you: Getting insights from young women with metastatic breast cancer. Unpublished survey. Atlanta: Young Survivor Coalition.

Rowe, J., M. Esser, S. Lewis, and M. McCann. 2014. Surveying young women with metastatic breast cancer to create interventions with impact. Poster presentation. Denver: BCY2 Conference.

Siegel, K., V. Gluhoski, and E. Gorey. 1999. Age related distress among young women with breast cancer. *Journal of Psychosocial Oncology* 17:1–20.

Stanton, A. L., and S. Danoff-Burg. 2002. Emotional expression, expressive writing and cancer. In *The writing cure: How expressive writing promotes health and emotional well-being*, edited by S. J. Lepore and J. M. Smyth, 31–51. Washington, DC: American Psychological Association.

Notes

1. Although we can arguably state that cancer survivors, in general, would agree that cancer is traumatic, this is statistically validated. See Hampton and Frombach (2000) and Mehnert and Koch (2007).

2. A drug used to treat certain types of breast cancer in women and men. It is also used to prevent breast cancer in women who have had ductal carcinoma in situ (abnormal cells in the ducts of the breast) and in women who are at a high risk of developing breast cancer. Tamoxifen is also being studied in the treatment of other types of cancer. It blocks the effects of the hormone estrogen in the breast.

Tamoxifen is a type of antiestrogen. Also called tamoxifen citrate. (National Cancer Institute 2012).

3. Changing the way one thinks and trying new behaviors is rooted in cognitive behavioral therapy (Cooper and Lesser 2002).

4. An example of a more in-depth study is a recent one conducted by the Young Survival Coalition (YSC) regarding its metastatic constituency (Rowe and Esser 2013).

One of the more important research questions identified by YSC for stage IV young breast cancer survivors is how their unique psychosocial needs are being met. See YSC Research Agenda, page 3, available at www.youngsurvival.org/research-agenda.

The YSC metastatic study categorized "emotional well-being" within the YSC metastatic survey. Participants were initially asked if this topic was important to them. If they answered no, they were moved to the next section of the survey. If they answered yes, they then answered questions about emotional impacts of diagnosis (including effects of cancer on sexuality, depression, anxiety, contemplation of end of life, etc.) and the accessibility of the healthcare provider team to help with emotional well-being, either directly or by referral.

The results of the survey revealed that 26 percent of participants spoke to no one about their emotional well-being, and only 44 percent of participants spoke to their medical oncologists about it (Rowe et al. 2014).

Other results revealed that 61 percent of participants spoke to no one about sex and intimacy; 73 percent spoke to no one regarding end-of-life planning; and 81 percent spoke to no one regarding being single and returning to the dating arena. These results are both sobering with regard to the lack of communication as well as highlighting an opportunity for improving patient care.

EPILOGUE

Honoring Silence

JEANNIE WRIGHT AND KATE THOMPSON

There is not one but many silences, and they are an integral part of the strategies that underlie and permeate discourses.

—Michel Foucault, *The History of Sexuality 1: An Introduction*

As we reach the end of this book, it is time to consider silence. As the writers of the preceding chapters fall silent, you may choose to break your own silence in writing.

There are many types of silence. Silence may be a gift or a deprivation, a choice or an oppression. In a therapy session we may sit in silence with a client and feel the deeper level of communication between us. We may choose silence and solitude to facilitate writing, or we may find that those conditions prevent us. Silence may be involuntary or a choice; there may be reasons for silence, for long gaps in keeping a journal. Here we look at what different silences in writing may mean and how we may honor or overcome them.

> Awake again at 4 AM. I can't blame anything going on at work, there's no noise nothing to wake me at all. It's irrational. Usually I would pick up the pen and start writing and that's what's most frustrating. The lights on, I'm sitting up, the room temperature is fine and I'm just staring at the wall. No words.
> —Tony, counseling client

Paradoxically, Tony's words are here on the page for us to read. Although he says he can't write, that no words are coming to the end of his pen, he is still talking to himself on the page. One of the extraordinarily powerful benefits of journal writing is the creative expression of the internal self-talk captured on the page. Capturing inner voices in writing enables rereading: It is more than record keeping. When we see our inner voices on the page, we can acknowledge these other parts of ourselves.

Another client, Sue, a lifelong journal keeper, found that, after the sudden death of her husband, she was unable to write in her journal. She was outraged and frightened by this loss of support at this time of huge loss and bereavement. She said she felt deserted by the practice she had always relied on to help her process and survive difficult times and experiences. There was a parallel process of the loss of two intimate relationships. Silence in the journal mirrored the silence in her life and represented the emotional vacuum of her grief.

We, Kate and Jeannie, are lifelong writers and also therapists and teachers. We know from our own experience the power of writing. We also know the dislocation of not writing. Both psychological and physical trauma can result in enforced silence. The process of finding language again and making it visible on the page is both slow and vital.

From Jeannie's Journal

I will draw on my own experience when, very occasionally, the writing to live that has stood me in such good stead since I was old enough to write fails me, or I fail it. Vanishes, dries up—none of these metaphors captures the shock. Recently, returning from a period of working and living in New Zealand for several years, my habitual way of capturing experience in writing just wasn't happening. During transitions between countries and jobs, during those life events like childbirth and bereavement writing has sustained me like nothing else. What might explain the not-writing periods of my life? What could the power of those silences be? (Wright 2009)

Protective Silence

Just as we might avoid touching a wound, some human experience leads to instinctive avoidance and inhibition. Traumatic memories seem best forgotten and can even lead to loss or suppression of memory and, in extreme circumstances, to some people being made mute. In Alice Walker's 1983 novel, *The Color Purple*, Celie, the protagonist, is rendered mute by her abuse as a child. Writing eventually helps her break her silence and reclaim her voice.

In the end breaking the silence is essential for healing. "Let us *speak* of this, you wisest men, even if it is a bad thing. To be silent is worse; all suppressed truths become poisonous" (Nietsche 1961, 139).

Sometimes society imposes silence, ostensibly to protect itself or those within it. Within Western cultures in a generalized way, it is not considered appropriate for those involved in the armed or emergency services to talk about their experience. Only recently have the talking therapies been introduced to the fire service, the armed services, for paramedics. In some cultures it is taboo to talk or to write about certain subjects. Trauma cannot be spoken of or written about for fear of harming others, or for fear of making it real. This silence is certainly intended to be protective, both for the writer or speaker and for the reader or listener.

In my (Kate's) work with trauma clients, I have found that some people can write about the traumatic event before they can speak about it. Sometimes writing helps them to break the silence imposed by trauma, break through the

From Kate's Journal

Having been a journal writer since I could make marks on the page, I found it extremely distressing to have a period in my teens when I could not write—I literally could not write—a neurological event utterly disrupted my mental and physical processes. The relearning was slow. I was unlanguaged and felt cut off from my very self when I could not write.

dissociation, and overcome the terror of the experience. However, this is a slow and delicate process and must be paced to the client's ability.

We need to honor the protective silence when it occurs in our clients or our own experience, trusting that words will return in their own time, perhaps when it is safe for them to do so. Sometimes they return little by little, a word or two at a time. Poetry can be easier than prose, the allusive and metaphorical more accessible than coherent description. Talking about not-writing in therapy sessions can be useful and encouraging permission to not-write is helpful.

I suggest clients write a list of "things I will not talk to Kate about." They are often delighted with both the permission and the idea of having secrets. The list of silences usually gets shorter over time.

On Not Writing

When writers can't write, when the ability to write deserts them, it can be very hard. Rainer (1978) suggests that these blocks or inabilities to write are caused by either the Internal Critic (fears about the style and quality of the writing) or the Internal Censor (fears about the legitimacy or acceptability of the content of the writing). This is equally true for personal journal writers as it is for professional writers. Whether it is process or product writing, the inability to write strikes at the heart of the writer's identity. When the writing voice is silenced for whatever reason, the striving to find it again can take many forms. These might include writing more or writing less, experimenting with techniques, or changing external environments.

One temptation might be to seek out more silence, which can have unexpected results. When writer Sara Maitland sought silence and isolation to deepen and improve her writing by moving to remote Weardale, in the north of England, she found something she described as "shocking":

> Now quite simply stories did not spring to mind; my imagination did not spring to mind. I had in a peculiarly literal way "lost the plot." I found this disturbing. More to the point I could not understand what was happening. . . .

Luckily I had already become aware that there are lots of sorts of silence. (Maitland 2008, 189–90)

Maitland drops further and further into silence, her own and others, and writes *A Book of Silence* (2008).

Natalie Goldberg suggests that silence can be a powerful facilitator for writing:

Behind writing, behind words is no words. We need to know about that place. It gives us a larger perspective from which to handle language. . . . Yes, silence can be an avoidance, a suppression, a way of hiding, a shyness, a secret that never gets examined, a solidification of the last heart. (Goldberg 2013, 9–10)

Thinking about the type of silence, being aware of the source of the silence, is important.

The Fear of Intrusion

Journal writers can be silenced by fears of having their journals read, by having their privacy violated.

I (Jeannie) worked with a client called Tamara in brief, workplace counseling. Tamara's losses were multiple and she found seeking help from counseling an extremely alien concept. She had not been able to speak about her bereavement. There were just three sessions left, and she hadn't found journal writing easy either.

"When am I going to do it?" Tamara asked. "If I start doing something at home, I'm always interrupted. I've done the shopping in my lunch hour from work, got the dinner ready, but my daughter needs a clean school shirt, so there's no time—and I forgot to collect my dad's prescription."

We laughed about a Victorian quotation on my office wall:

Happy women do not write . . . their lives are rounded and complete, they require nothing but a calm recurrence of those peaceful home duties in which domestic women rightly feel their true vocation lies. (Hamilton 1892, 13)

From *Women Writers, Their Works and Ways*, 1892, this vision of a calm domesticity couldn't have been more different from Tamara's hectic juggling.

More important than not finding the time, Tamara was cautious about expressing herself on paper. She was stopped by the sense that once thoughts and feelings were outside of her own head and on paper, others could access them. "It doesn't feel safe," she said. As we shall soon see, Tamara was able to find a way to break her silence.

One of my (Kate's) clients always wrote and kept her journal in her car. It was the only space that was truly hers and where she felt safe and not overlooked. When she was in the house there was always someone making demands on her. Writing in her parked car on the way to or from therapy became her refuge.

In some situations people are required to keep journals and they may find this difficult. Trainee therapists, for example, who are required to keep personal development journals, may find the idea that their journal is to be read unpalatable and may therefore silence themselves. Overcoming this silence of writing can be crucial for their academic success. Some anxious students say, "I don't need to write things down. I keep my ideas, emotions, and thoughts in my head." A useful bridge is the reflection write, a narrative that takes a meta-view of the private journal entry and asks for focus on the process, insights, somatic sensations and "aha" moments of the *process* of writing (Sawyer 2013).

Overcoming Silence

Writing to a Trusted and Nonjudgmental Presence

In my (Jeannie's) experience as a therapist, and essentially in my own use of journal writing, I have found that expressing something to a nonjudgmental person, to write to a warm, empathic presence, can start the flow (Wright and Bolton 2012).

This person can be real and known in the past or present: a mentor, coach, counselor, friend, relative, teacher. The presence might also be virtual and imagined, perhaps a part of the writer's self. There might also be a spiritual depth in this imagined presence, as we saw with Celie's letters to God in *The Color Purple* (Walker 1983). Some people suggest that imagining a reader is a vital part of the healing power of writing; I would add that this is much easier when the imagined reader is one who is trustworthy and reliable.

This idea enabled my client Tamara to overcome her silence and fears about writing her journal. She described how years ago in her youth, a teacher had taken particular interest in her. The teacher had not judged her for her less-than-ideal family of origin. She was open to the idea that an "unsent letter" to this teacher, essentially telling the story she had a hard time telling me, would be worth trying.

What Tamara discovered in the unsent letter was rage. She chose not to read me the letter in our next session. In fact, she could barely meet my eyes and seemed unusually slow to get started. When she spoke about how the writing had uncovered bitter and angry feelings toward the people she'd lost as well as the people who were still here, her face and neck turned redder until eventually she covered her face with her hands. She said she was ashamed of the acid in her letter and didn't know she could feel like that.

We talked about what to do with the letter. Tamara said she wanted to destroy it. She tore it up with gritted teeth and seemed relieved. Her shoulders dropped. She said she was exhausted and was glad it was the end of the day and could go home instead of into work afterward.

Suggesting to students in counseling courses that they write their journal as unsent letters to a warm and nonjudgmental presence is one way to break into the empty screen or the fear of the blank sheets of paper. For humanistic students and practitioners, envisaging a presence that embodies Carl Rogers's (1980) core conditions is a helpful way in.

The War Poets and Silence

In Britain in 2014 the one hundredth anniversary of the outbreak of the First World War was commemorated in different ways.

Poets have different ways to distill experience and to communicate it. In the historical novels comprising *The Regeneration Trilogy* (1996), author Pat Barker considers traumatic experience in war and its impact, including being

> ## From Jeannie's Journal
>
> Within my own family, in a British cultural tradition of "mustn't grumble" and "stiff upper lip," my grandparents' experience of the first war and my parents' memories of the Second World War were never disclosed, or only in sanitized ways, using "gallows humor" to distance the emotion.

rendered mute, an extreme of silence. The novels are based on the actual in-hospital treatment for shell shock of two famous war poets, Siegfried Sassoon and Wilfred Owen, by the anthropologist-turned-psychiatrist William Rivers. Barker weaves powerful themes in which both expression and silence are seen to be protective.

In one of the most harrowing passages, a soldier who has been rendered mute by his experiences in the trenches is given electric shocks to force him to speak, by a doctor, not Rivers, who appears to be less humane in his practice than any ethical code of conduct would permit. The only way to stop the torture of repeated shocks is for the soldier to speak.

The poet Siegfried Sassoon left a written account of his experience on the front line in the First World War, including being shot at the Battle of Arras and everyday survival in the trenches. The archive of twenty-three journals and two notebooks of poetry has been digitized by the Cambridge University Library, which bought the collection in 2009. Had Sassoon suffered the kind of silence that sometimes arises from trauma, he would not have been able to draw upon his immediate expression of the unspeakable in order to craft his poetry.

In many ways this is the counterargument to silence as protection. Sassoon, a dedicated diarist, perhaps survived as well as he did psychologically because of his ability to communicate in words and drawings, describing the Battle of the Somme as a "sunlit picture of hell" (Sassoon 2013). Those fragile and mud-stained notebooks and diaries are now available to be read on the Internet anywhere in the world.

The Gift of Silence

But sometimes the writing muscle needs to rest, just like a body that has been pushed to exertion for too long; sometimes people need a break from writing, from thinking, from themselves. This is when the ability to choose a transient silence is a gift. During the break something else can happen, perhaps just being involved in doing things, of living in the world. Silence may provide an essential breathing space within the dialogue with the self, a pause before meaning is revealed. Perhaps this break is what makes it possible for the next phase of understanding to occur. Silence is an invitation to listen, either to ourselves or the world around us.

References

Barker, Pat. 1996. *The regeneration trilogy*. New York: Viking.

Goldberg, Natalie. 2013. *The true secret of writing*. New York: Atria.

Hamilton, Catherine J. 1892. *Women writers; their works and ways*. London: Ward, Lock, Bowden & Co.

Maitland, Sara. 2008. *A book of silence: A journey in search of the pleasures and powers of silence*. London: Granta Books.

Nietsche, Friedrich. 1961. *Thus spoke Zarathustra*. London: Penguin.

Rainer, Tristine. 1978. *The new diary*. Los Angeles: Jeremy P. Tarcher.

Rogers, Carl. 1980. *A way of being*. Boston: Houghton Mifflin.

Sassoon, Siegfried. 2013. *Memoirs of an infantry officer*. London: Penguin.

Sawyer, Joy Roulier. 2013. Liberating beauty. In *Expressive writing: Foundations of practice*, edited by K. Adams. Lanham, MD: Rowman & Littlefield.

Walker, Alice. 1983. *The color purple*. London: The Women's Press.

Wright, Jeannie K. 2009. Autoethnography and therapy: Writing on the move. *Qualitative Inquiry* 15(4):623–40.

Wright, Jeannie K., and Gillie Bolton. 2012. *Reflective writing in counselling and psychotherapy*. London: Sage.

About the Editors and Contributors

Editors

Kate Thompson, MA, CJT, is an existential psychotherapist, certified journal therapist, teacher, and writer. A lifelong journal writer, it was natural to her to integrate writing into psychotherapy for the benefit of clients and colleagues. She pioneered the use of journal writing in individual counseling and for self-supervision in the United Kingdom. Kate is the author of *Therapeutic Journal Writing: An Introduction for Professionals* (2010) and coeditor of *Writing Works* (2006) and *Writing Routes* (2010). Kate grew up in Yorkshire and now lives in the Rocky Mountains of Boulder, Colorado. Landscape has always been an inspiration for her work, her life, and her writing. She is core faculty for the Therapeutic Writing Institute.

Kathleen Adams, LPC, PTR-M/S, is the founding director and chief executive officer of the Center for Journal Therapy, Inc. headquartered in Denver, Colorado. In 2008 she opened the center's online professional training division, the Therapeutic Writing Institute, and in 2013 she added an online membership community, the Journalverse. She has been a pioneer, visionary, and guide in the field of therapeutic writing since 1985. This is her eleventh book.

Contributors

Christina Baldwin (foreword) is the author of three groundbreaking works on writing, *One to One, Self Understanding through Journal Writing* (1971), *Life's Companion, Journal Writing as a Spiritual Practice,* (1991, rev. 2007), and *Storycatcher, Making Sense of our Lives through the Power and Practice of Story* (2007). She has taught a seminar on creative nonfiction, "The Self as the Source of the Story," since 1989, www.peerspirit.com.

John F. Evans, MAT, MA, EdD (chapter 3) is a writing clinician and certified integrative health coach, writer, and speaker. He is founder and executive director of Wellness & Writing Connections, LLC and provides individual, group, and institutional life course guidance programs for health care providers and their clients. With James Pennebaker, Evans coauthored *Expressive Writing: Words That Heal* (2014). His book, *Wellness & Writing Connections: Writing for Better Physical, Mental, and Spiritual Health* (2010), is a collection of essays from the Wellness & Writing Connections Conference Series.

Victoria Field, CAPF, M/S (chapter 1) is a writer, certified poetry therapist, and approved mentor/supervisor based in Canterbury, United Kingdom. She is coeditor of three books about therapeutic writing, most recently *Writing Routes* (2010). Victoria teaches and trains internationally and is a past chair of Lapidus. She has won awards for her poetry, fiction, and drama, including her most recent collection *The Lost Boys* (2013) and has been commissioned by BBC Radio 3 and 4. She blogs at www.poetrytherapynews.com.

Graham Hartill (chapter 1) is currently writer-in-residence at one of Britain's largest prisons. He teaches in the *Creative Writing for Therapeutic Purposes* MSc program at the Metanoia Institute in London and Bristol. In 2013 he was the first writer-in-residence at Swansea University College of Medicine and, with Victoria Field, runs a popular course, *Writing in Health and Social Care,* at Ty Newydd, the Writers' Centre for Wales.

Donna Houston (chapter 8) is a licensed School Counselor at the Iowa School for the Deaf. She is also a certified Speech & Language Pathologist and

Teacher of the Deaf. Having worked with deaf and hard-of-hearing teenagers since 1992, she has found the most rewarding aspect of her work is bringing the healing power of written expression to high school students, especially those for whom literacy is a challenge.

Beth Jacobs, PhD (chapter 5) is a lifetime journaler and clinical psychologist who has studied and supported the profound therapeutic powers of writing. She is author of *Writing for Emotional Balance* and *Paper Sky: What Happened after Anne Franks's Diary Ended*, as well as a columnist (The Journaler's Corner) for the National Association for Poetry Therapy's *Museletter*.

Karen Jooste, MD (chapter 3) is a pediatrician, teacher, coach, and workshop leader. She practices pediatrics at Duke Pediatrics Primary Care and teaches medical students in the Practice Course (clinical skills and medical humanities) at Duke University School of Medicine. As the founder of Storia International PLLC she fuses her passions for medicine and writing through coaching and workshops designed to facilitate vibrant wellness and resilience.

Meredith Mealer, RN, PhD (chapter 3) is associate professor at the University of Colorado–Denver Medical School, Division of Pulmonary Science and Critical Care. She has previously published on posttraumatic stress disorder and burnout syndrome in nurses.

Marc Moss, MD (chapter 3) is professor of medicine and section head of critical care medicine at the University of Colorado–Denver Medical School, Division of Pulmonary Science and Critical Care. He is the 2011 recipient of the president's award, American Thoracic Society.

Susan Smith Pierce, PhD, LPCC (chapter 9) is the director of professional development and coordinator of clinical internships at Southwest Family Guidance Center and Institute in Albuquerque, New Mexico. Dr. Smith Pierce is a certified Journal to the Self instructor and teaches workshops in expressive writing and self-care for mental health clinicians. Prior to her work at Southwest Family Guidance Center, she was a counseling professor at the University of New Mexico and directed the on-site clinical training center.

Sherry Reiter, PhD, PTR (chapter 4) is a clinical social worker and registered poetry therapist who combines talk therapy with writing therapy. As director of the Creative "Righting" Center in Brooklyn, she focuses on poetry, story, and the reclaiming of voice as dynamic healing components. She is the author of *Writing Away the Demons: Stories of Creative Coping Through Transformative Writing* (2009), stories by men and women who have faced crisis and written for their psychological survival. Sherry teaches at Touro College and Hofstra University.

Carol Ross (chapter 7) has been working as a writing practitioner in the UK National Health Service since 2009. She leads weekly therapeutic writing sessions for patients in several mental health wards in Cumbria in the United Kingdom. She edited and coauthored *Words for Wellbeing*, an anthology of chapters, poetry, and prose, and has had a number of articles, stories, and poems published.

Deborah Ross LPC, CJT (chapter 2) studied Interpersonal Neurobiology at the Mindsight Institute with Dr. Dan Siegel and applied her findings to therapeutic writing. An avid journaler, she recognizes the healing power of expressive writing and believes that this practice can change the way our brains work so that we experience a deeper sense of well-being and great resilience. Deborah is a licensed psychotherapist and a certified journal therapist (Therapeutic Writing Institute). Her first book, *Your Brain on Ink*, is a workbook coauthored with Kathleen Adams for this expressive writing series. She teaches at the Therapeutic Writing Institute.

Jean Rowe, LCSW, CJT (chapter 11) is a certified journal therapist (Therapeutic Writing Institute) and licensed clinical social worker certified in oncology. She is the associate director of survivorship programs for the Young Survival Coalition, where she specializes in providing counseling, support, and resources to young women affected by breast cancer. Jean leads an original writing program addressing reestablishing intimacy after cancer and has also provided original journal groups for Winship Cancer Institute of Emory University and continuing education journal writing programs for mental health and healthcare professionals.

Cherie Spehar, LCSW, CTC-S, RPT-S (chapter 6) is the founder/director and lead clinician of Smiling Spirit Pathways/The Apex Center for Trauma Healing LLC, an award-winning trauma-informed practice in North Carolina. She is a registered play therapist and supervisor who is among the first to combine play therapy with journal therapy. Cherie is also the lead blogger, weekly columnist, and certified department trainer for The National Institute for Trauma and Loss in Children. She provides educational workshops, presentations, consultations, and trauma-informed speaking engagements locally and nationally on a monthly basis.

Barbara Stahura, CJF (chapter 10) is a freelance writer/editor and certified journal facilitator (Therapeutic Writing Institute) who has been facilitating journaling workshops for people with brain injury and with family caregivers since 2007, first in Arizona and now in Indiana. She is also coauthor with Susan B. Schuster, MA, CCC-SLP, of *After Brain Injury: Telling Your Story*, the acclaimed first journaling book for people with brain injury. She speaks nationally on journaling for these populations and is on the faculty of the Therapeutic Writing Institute.

Jeannie Wright, PhD (epilogue) has written what she cannot say since she was very young and has maintained the habit. She has worked as therapist, clinical supervisor, and educator in the United Kingdom, New Zealand, and most memorably, Fiji. Her publications, books, and articles focus on the therapeutic benefits of creative and reflective writing. This remains her major interest in research.

Acknowledgments

From Kate

First, I want to express my gratitude to my coeditor, inspiration, and friend, Kay Adams. I want to acknowledge the fun, inspiration, and learning we've shared in the process of taking this book from wisps of ideas to the volume we have here. It has been a wonderful journey.

Thank you to the many colleagues old and new who have contributed to this book—those of you who have written chapters and patiently shaped and developed the work, those of you who have offered wise words in discussion and conversation during this process project, and those of you who have read drafts at different stages and provided valuable feedback. It is a privilege to belong to such a vibrant community and to contribute to its growth.

As always, my clients, supervisees, and students take me into new areas of the work and bring fresh insights to what I know. They are the ones who keep me passionate about this field. My approach to this work owes more to them than I can say.

Thank you to our publishers and the individuals there who have worked with us and continually encouraged this project.

Thanks always to Michael who supports each project I undertake with patience.

Kate Thompson

From Kay

Kate Thompson and I have successfully collaborated on many projects over the years, and I think we reached a new pinnacle with this book. Thanks, Kate, for marathon sessions on the mountain, your brilliant editorial eye, the fun, the gallons of coffee. I've loved coediting with you!

Much gratitude to the book's editorial review board, Vanessa Jackson, Peggy Osna Heller, and Linda Barnes. Your suggestions made this book shine.

Thanks to Sarah Jubar, editor; Carlie Wall, associate editor; Dean Roxanis, marketing manager; Maria Kaufman, cover designer; and the entire R&L Education team for making this series possible, and for being great to work with.

I'm grateful to my accountability partner, Mary Reynolds Thompson, who once again helped me incubate ideas, tasks, and outcomes on this project, and to Leia Francisco, my business coach, whose steady presence grounds my vision and lights the path.

To the Journal to the Self instructor community, the Therapeutic Writing Institute student body and alumni, the Journalverse membership, and the wide global circle of those who know and appreciate the work of the Center for Journal Therapy: You are the present and the future of this work. My gratitude is endless.

I was born into a family I would choose all over again as friends, and their love is constant and deep. Thanks, Susie, Cindy, Leo, and all who call me Aunt Kay.

Finally, I give thanks for having been given wonderful work to do and wonderful people with whom to do it. It is my joy.

Kathleen Adams